FANTASTIC STOMPS
AROUND GREAT BRITAIN

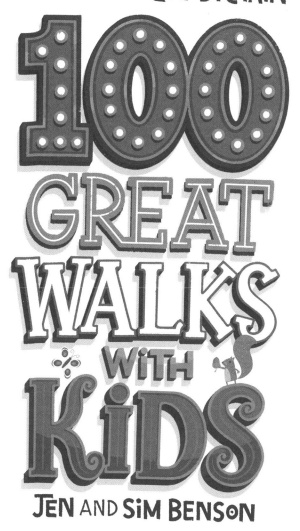

100
GREAT
WALKS
WITH
KiDS

JEN AND SiM BENSON

C◈NWAY
LONDON · OXFORD · NEW YORK · NEW DELHI · SYDNEY

CONWAY
Bloomsbury Publishing Plc
50 Bedford Square, London, WC1B 3DP, UK

BLOOMSBURY, CONWAY and the Conway logo are trademarks of Bloomsbury Publishing Plc

First published in 2021

ISBN: PB: 978-1-8448-6575-8; eBook: 978-1-8448-6577-2; ePDF: 978-1-8448-6576-5

10 9 8 7 6 5 4 3 2 1

Typeset in Myriad Pro by Phil Beresford
Printed and bound in India by Replika Press Pvt. Ltd.

MIX
Paper from
responsible sources
FSC® C016779

To find out more about our authors and books visit www.bloomsbury.com and sign up for our newsletters

Note: while every effort has been made to ensure the accuracy of this guidebook, changes can
occur over time. If you discover any important changes to the details in this book, we're happy
to hear about them Please send any comments to adlardcoles@bloomsbury.com

CONTENTS

Introduction **9**
About this book **12**

SOUTH WEST ENGLAND

SOUTH EAST ENGLAND

CENTRAL ENGLAND AND EAST ANGLIA

NORTH ENGLAND

WALES

SCOTLAND

INTRODUCTION

Walking – as a family, extended family or group of friends – is a fantastic way to spend time together. Far from the urban and indoors worlds that so many of us, and our children, spend much of our lives inhabiting, walking outdoors in all weathers and on every kind of terrain brings a level of exhilaration, engagement and immersion in our surroundings that occurs nowhere else. Getting outside and sharing the challenges, joys, sights and sounds of a place with other people forms bonds and memories that last a lifetime.

Walks are almost always an education, but not the kind you'll find sitting in a classroom. A walk can explore the history of the Earth through its rocks, or the history of humans by visiting the places where people have left their mark, from remains in caves and hilltop forts to castles and country estates. Every wild place is buzzing with its own unique blend of nature – from birds and mammals to the tiny worlds of invertebrates. Gazing up at the dark skies that hang speckled with stars over many of Britain's National Parks is a magical way to learn about the universe and our place within it. Seeing conservation projects in action, and the changes – both good and bad – happening across so many of our landscapes, brings immediacy and relevance to issues such as climate change, biodiversity and land use.

THE DOORSTEP MILE

Every child is different, with some relishing the idea of going for a walk while others will do anything to avoid it. Regardless of age or inclination, forcing kids to go on walks does little besides creating tension and conflict, and you'll end up never wanting to do it again. Getting kids on board with the idea of a walk really is all about how you pitch it to them. If you can, get them involved in planning the day. Is there anywhere they'd really like to go? What are they learning about at school that could be enhanced by seeing it in real life? Do they have any special interests, such as steam trains or rock climbing? And, often most importantly, is there a café at the finish where you can all enjoy a hot chocolate together?

It's often hard for children to imagine the day ahead, particularly if it's somewhere they've never been before, so waymarking it with more familiar things that they know they enjoy helps them to understand what's going to happen and why it'll be fun. Arranging to meet their friends for a walk is a fantastic way to combine something they're likely to find exciting with getting outside and exploring. However you go about it, even if the distance covered is exactly the same, kids will always view an 'adventure' with far more enthusiasm than a 'walk'.

SEASONAL VARIATIONS

Nature can be a great guide when it comes to planning walks. Beech woods blaze with colour and woodland floors are filled with fascinating fungi in autumn. Snowdrops appear in early spring, with primroses, daffodils and bluebells soon after. Winter brings its own special type of fun, from muddy puddles to ice crystals and even snow. On a hot summer's day, a shady trail alongside a stream is perfect for cooling down with a paddle and brings a whole new perspective from which to spot wildlife. In late summer, foraging for blackberries from the hedgerows and bilberries from forests and mountainsides is a great way to sow the seeds of self-sufficiency, and an excellent source of free, healthy and delicious snacks as you go.

FOOTWEAR AND CLOTHING

Children are literally finding their feet when they start out, so footwear is one of the most important considerations when it comes to helping them to build the foundations for a life of confident and enjoyable outdoor exploration. Shoes or boots should fit well, have excellent grip and be breathable or waterproof enough for the conditions. A good pair of socks – Merino wool is perfect where possible – will add warmth, breathability and comfort to any pair of shoes.

When it comes to clothing, choose multiple lightweight layers that can be added or removed as required. Children vary much more than adults in their activity levels and lose heat more rapidly, so easy clothing adjustment is important. A good waterproof to go over the top of everything – all-in-ones work brilliantly for younger children while a jacket and salopette-style trousers are ideal when they're bigger – keeps everything as dry and clean as possible.

BUGGIES AND CARRIERS

Walking with really young children is a great way for new parents to get outside and spend some much-needed quality time together. A good off-road buggy with suspension, rugged tyres and decent brakes can make a walk in the woods an enjoyable excursion, and the good ones will handle rough terrain with ease. Many shops will let you take one out on a trial run – essential for making sure it works for all of you – and there's usually a wide selection available second-hand.

Our own adventures take us up mountains and over stiles, so we opted for baby carriers when our kids were little. If you find the frame-style carriers a little heavy and bulky, it's well worth giving the softer, structured carriers such as the Ergobaby a try. These can be worn on the front, back or side and keep the child close so you can monitor – and share – body heat. They also enable you to carry your child's weight close to your centre of mass, which is efficient and safer over rough terrain. Soft carriers and slings pack small enough to fit easily into a rucksack and, if you're up for carrying them, will transport a child up to around the age of four, so they're a useful item to take along on a walk in case a child wants to be carried any distance. You can also buy warm and/or waterproof covers that provide an excellent level of protection for the child.

FIRST AID AND TICKS

A basic first aid kit – including antiseptic wipes, plasters in a range of sizes, absorbent dressings, bite/sting relief, tweezers, tick removers, small scissors and some micropore tape – is well worth keeping in your pack for those inevitable minor bumps and grazes that happen on days out with kids. Ticks are increasingly common in Britain's outdoors and they carry a range of nasty diseases that can transmit to humans when they bite. They can be found all year round in urban or rural environments across the country in damp, wildlife-rich areas, particularly in mid-length to long grass. Bites are painless but the longer the tick is attached, the higher the chances of disease transmission, so if you or your child does get bitten it's important to remove the tick promptly. Use a specifically designed tick-removal tool to avoid distressing the tick or leaving its mouth parts in the skin. Being careful to stick to paths, avoiding likely spots and tick checking everyone regularly is essential – look for a small black or brown seed-like creature, attached firmly to the skin. If you notice a red circular rash or flu-like symptoms after someone has received a tick bite, see your GP.

SHARED RIGHTS OF WAY

While the vast majority of walks included in this book follow public footpaths, some also take in stretches of bridleway, byway and quiet road. These rights of way may be shared with horses, cyclists and motor vehicles, so take extra care, particularly when walking with younger children. Many paths are also popular with dog walkers. If you're bringing a dog, check in advance for location-specific guidelines as these often vary throughout the year in places such as beaches and conservation areas. Dogs are great company on walks but can easily scare or harm wildlife, fragile habitats, livestock and other people; responsible dog ownership is good for everyone.

THE COUNTRYSIDE CODE

The Countryside Code is all about respecting, protecting and enjoying the outdoors. It's a great way for kids to learn to adventure responsibly and help take care of the places they visit.

The Code asks us all to:

- **Enjoy the outdoors.**
- **Respect other people.**
- **Consider the local community and other people enjoying the outdoors.**
- **Leave gates and property as you find them.**
- **Keep to paths.**
- **Protect the natural environment.**
- **Leave no trace of your visit and take your litter home.**
- **Keep dogs under effective control.**
- **Plan ahead and be prepared.**
- **Follow advice and local signs.**

ABOUT THIS BOOK

The walks in this book all start in the same place as they finish, for ease of logistics. While most follow circular routes, there are a few that go out and back where we feel this gives the best quality of walk. These are mainly our 'mini mountain' walks, where the first half is spent climbing up to a summit and the second half enjoying the gravity-assisted walk back down again. From experience, we've found this a very popular format with children, where an achievable goal is at the top of the hill – perhaps with a stop for snacks and exploring along the way – while the tired miles are all downhill.

Accompanying each walk you'll find useful information about the surrounding area and suggestions for other kid-friendly places to visit while you're there.

The following symbols are used throughout the book:

 Buggy/wheelchair friendly – suitable for an all-terrain buggy or wheelchair

 Dog friendly or partly dog friendly – those locations where dogs are not allowed or only at certain times of the year

 Refreshments – family-friendly cafes, pubs and kiosks, which includes takeaway-only establishments

 Toilets – public toilets available

 Hazard – trickier walks and those with busy road crossings, cliff edges or other similar hazards. The specific nature of the hazard is explained within the details for the walk

 Beach – walk passes or crosses a family-friendly beach

FINDING YOUR WAY

Every walk in this book has been carefully chosen with family-friendly navigation in mind. It is intended that the map and step-by-step directions included will be sufficient for finding your way in clear conditions. We highly recommend purchasing an OS 1:25,000 Explorer map for any areas you will be spending time in. Detailing every footpath and bridleway, these are a great way for everyone to get started in the art of navigation, planning routes and following along as you go. There are also many excellent apps and online resources for route planning and navigation.

THE WALKS

SOUTH WEST ENGLAND

Wild beaches and whale tales on Bryher

BRYHER, ISLES OF SCILLY

Bryher is the smallest of the five inhabited islands of Scilly, a scattered archipelago in the Atlantic Ocean, some 28 miles (45km) off the coast of mainland Cornwall. A place that balances wild and rugged features with the friendly warmth of the people, its beautiful beaches, few cars and inquisitive wildlife make it a wonderful spot to explore with children of any age. It has also been an inspiration for writers; the 1985 book *Why the Whales Came* by Michael Morpurgo is set on the island during the First World War and relates the adventures of two young friends who lived there.

Away from the main town area, most of the walking on Bryher follows grassy paths and tracks, with some rocky sections. Our walk here follows the coastline, which is easy to navigate and takes in all of its incredible variety, from sandy beaches to rugged cliffs. To the north, you'll discover Shipman Head, home to dramatic seascapes and a high, rocky promontory, while the coastline along Bryher's eastern edge has great views across Hangman Island to neighbouring Tresco. The best beaches lie around the south-west of the island, including the peaceful shingle of Popplestones and the fine white sands of Rushy Bay, which is perfect for swimming and sandcastling. Friendly Bryher Campsite is a perfect base from which to explore the island.

WALK DETAILS

Start/finish: Bar quay, Bryher, TR23 0PR

Distance: 3.6 miles (5.8km)

Difficulty: 2/5

Public transport: Trains to Penzance, then catch the *Scillonian III* ferry to St Mary's, the largest island. Regular ferries run from St Mary's to Bryher and the other islands

DIRECTIONS

1. Leave the beach at Bar and turn right through the boatyard and right again following the path heading north to the coast. You'll pass Watch Hill to your left – the highest point on Bryher and well worth the hike to the top, where you'll find a former lookout and great views across the islands.

2. Continue north, passing the Fraggle Rock Bar and following the coast with the sea on your right along the Tresco Channel. Between Bryher and Tresco stands Hangman's Island, which is said to have been used for executions during the English Civil War.

3. Continuing north, you'll cross Shipman Head Down, home to one of the largest Bronze Age burial sites in north-western Europe and a great place from which to watch the waves rolling in from the vast Atlantic Ocean. The rocks of Shipman Head beyond are an important seabird breeding ground where you might spot herring gulls, great and lesser black-backed gulls, razorbills, fulmars, Manx shearwaters and, occasionally, ringed plovers and oystercatchers.

4. Tracing the western edge of the island southwards takes you past the sheltered bay at Popplestones, so called for the sound of the waves on the shingle shore. Just to the north of Popplestones is the longest cave in Scilly. Caution: with its narrow opening and tidal access, exploring is not recommended.

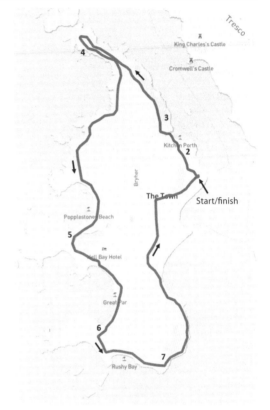

5. Continuing south from Popplestones, you'll skirt the edge of Great Pool – created through the excavation of peat for heating houses – and Gweal Hill, another worthy ascent for picnics or sunsets. There's a freshwater well at the foot of the hill; see if you can find it in the right-hand corner of the bottom field, near to a ruined house.

6. The next section takes you around Heathy Hill and past Droppy Nose Point. Look out for seals bobbing in the waves or hauled out on the rocks as you go. Cross the sands at Rushy Bay – a stunningly beautiful, sheltered beach that's ideal for swimming and paddling – and then carry on around Samson Hill at the far southern end of Bryher, passing the remains of a Cromwellian battery at Works Point.

7. Make your way back through town to return to the quay.

THINGS TO SEE AND DO NEARBY

Try some local delicacies, including Scilly-made ice cream, fudge, tatty cake and locally caught seafood.

Regular ferries run between all the inhabited islands. Explore the castles and world-renowned **Abbey Garden on Tresco**, take a boat trip from **St Mary's** to see seals and puffins on the uninhabited islands, or hire bikes or kayaks to explore the land and water further afield.

Sandy coves and Morse code at Poldhu

LIZARD, CORNWALL

The west coast of Cornwall's Lizard Peninsula, much of which is looked after by the National Trust, covers an incredible variety of scenery, from the Penrose estate with its expansive freshwater pool and manor house southwards along the rugged coastline to Mullion. Here, the peaceful, sandy coves are great to visit at any time of year, with a perfect mix of sandcastling and paddling for younger children, surfing for the more adventurous, and a cafe for everyone. This walk follows the South West Coast Path from Winnianton Farm, crossing the sandy, rock-edged beaches at Church Cove and Poldhu Cove and reaching the Poldhu Wireless Station, which, in 1901, transmitted the first trans-Atlantic wireless telegraphy signal, to Newfoundland, some 1,800 miles (2,900km) away.

This part of Cornwall is also special for its intriguing rock formations, a remnant of ancient oceans. Unlike most of the county, which lies on a bedrock of rough grey granite and smooth grey slate, much of the Lizard Peninsula is formed from a fascinating rock called serpentinite. This rare dark green-and-red rock, formed from a mixture of dark igneous gabbro and stripy metamorphic amphibolite, has been weathered to a shine over thousands of years and resembles the skin of a snake.

WALK DETAILS

Start/finish: Winnianton Farm National Trust Car Park, Gunwalloe, TR12 7QE

Distance: 2.5 miles (4km)

Difficulty: 2/5

Public transport: Bus stop at Poldhu linking Redruth, Helston, Mullion and Lizard

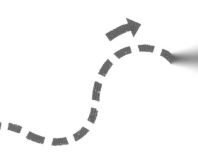

DIRECTIONS

1. From the car park, cross the road to reach the South West Coast Path. Turn left and follow the coast path with the sea on your right.

2. You'll soon pass the pretty church of St Winwaloe, the only church in Cornwall that stands on a beach. Cross the sands at Church Cove and climb back up to the coast path on the opposite side.

3. Cross the next stretch of headland and then descend to the beach at Poldhu Cove. A popular beach with families and surfers over the summer months, there is RNLI lifeguard cover every day between May and September.

4. Cross the beach to reach the road at Poldhu Car Park. Turn right, following signs for the coast path and Marconi Centre to reach the headland at Poldhu Point. It's well worth spending some time exploring here, visiting the Marconi Centre (see below) and monument and taking in the glorious coastal views.

5. Return to Winnianton Farm via your outward route or, at quieter times, explore the peaceful lanes and footpaths that loop inland, for a circular walk.

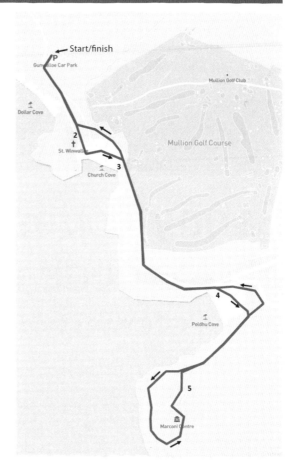

Start/finish
P
Gunwalloe Car Park
Mullion Golf Club
Dollar Cove
Mullion Golf Course
2
St. Winwaloe
3
Church Cove
4
Poldhu Cove
5
Marconi Centre

THINGS TO SEE AND DO NEARBY

The Marconi Centre, staffed by local volunteers, is a fascinating place to explore and learn about the origins of radio. Children can even earn a certificate by tapping out their name in Morse code.
Further south, **Kynance Cove** and **Lizard Point** are both beautiful, dramatic coastal features, while to the north, the National Trust's **Penrose** estate offers good, level walks, suitable for buggies, and the fascinating freshwater **Loe Pool**.

Caves and mines at Chapel Porth

ST AGNES, CORNWALL

It may be tiny and relatively undiscovered compared with many of Cornwall's beaches, but Chapel Porth and its surrounding area is a treasure trove of fascinating sights to discover and is wonderful for walking. Any visit should either begin or end on the beach, watching the waves roll in, scrambling up the rocky stacks and exploring the deep caves that run with cascades of water. At low tide, you can spot the boiler of the SS *Eltham*, a steamer that was wrecked here during storms in 1928.

Chapel Porth was a busy copper and tin mining area until the end of the 19th century and the place would have been dotted with heaps of spoil, mine workings and wooden huts and sheds, some of which are still visible. Nature has, for the most part, covered over the past and you can now find trees such as willow, sycamore, blackthorn and elder growing along the rising valley of Chapel Coombe. Over the summer months, keep an eye (and ear) out for birds here, including wrens, warblers, stonechats and chaffinches during the day and rare greater horseshoe bats that emerge from the mineshafts at dusk.

This walk showcases some of St Agnes' finest coastal scenery, with all of the ascent taking place in the first half and a long, downhill finish back to the beach.

WALK DETAILS

Start/finish: Chapel Porth National Trust Car Park, Chapel Porth, TR5 0NS

Distance: 2.5 miles (4km)

Difficulty: 3/5

Public transport: Bus service from Redruth train station stops at the Victory Inn in Towan Cross

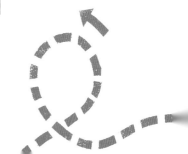

DIRECTIONS

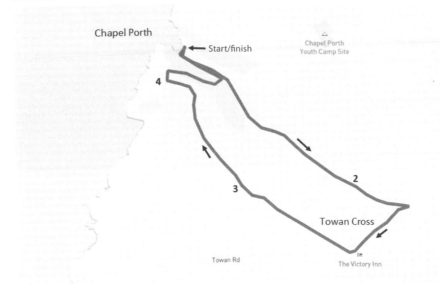

Chapel Porth

◄— Start/finish

Chapel Porth
Youth Camp Site

4

2

3

Towan Cross

Towan Rd

The Victory Inn

1 Start at the rear of the car park, then follow the footpath just to the right of the cafe. Cross over the footbridge and head away from the sea up the narrow valley of Chapel Coombe. Take care to keep to the path as the heather- and gorse-covered slopes hide the remnants of the area's mining history, including mineshafts and spoil heaps. As you reach the Charlotte United engine house towards the top of the hill you may spot orange staining on the soil and plants, caused by iron hydroxide being washed from the mines.

2 Continue on the footpath until you reach a minor road. Turn right here and follow the road through the hamlet of Towan Cross until you reach a junction opposite the Victory Inn. Turn right here and follow the road for a short distance, keeping to the verge, until you can turn right on to a bridleway signed to Porthtowan. Follow this towards the sea.

3 Where the bridleway forks, stay right, following the path across the heathland towards the ruins of Great Wheal Charlotte, a former copper mine that was used by US troops during the Second World War for target practice. Continue along the path to reach the headland summit of Mulgram Hill, from which you'll see glorious coastal views on a clear day.

4 Turn right and follow the wide track, known locally as the American Road, as it zigzags down the headland towards Chapel Porth, turning left at the path junction at the bottom to return to the car park.

THINGS TO SEE AND DO NEARBY

Chapel Porth has a long history of belly boarding and hosted the **World Belly Board Championships** between 2003 and 2015. The championships have now moved along the St Agnes coast to Perranporth, but the sport is a great introduction to surfing and a lot of fun.

Around the ruin at Rame Head

RAME, CORNWALL

Nestled on the south-easternmost edge of Cornwall, the distinctive chapel-topped headland at Rame is a wild, adventurous place, ideal for running around and exploring or simply watching the busy bustle of ships coming and going in Plymouth Sound. The vistas to the west are outstanding too, stretching out along the rugged Cornish coastline. It's for these views that Rame Head has long been used as a lookout, from the Celtic warriors who built a defensive rampart across the peninsula to defend it from possible attack to the medieval monks who kept a beacon burning to warn ships away from the rocks. Parts of the intriguing little chapel, dedicated to St German, date back to 1259.

This walk follows a short loop around the headland, tackling the steep flight of steps to reach the chapel. It's well worth taking some time to explore here and admire the views. On a clear day, you can see the Eddystone Lighthouse, 9 miles (14.5km) offshore. The Rame Peninsula is also a great place to spot magnificent birds of prey, including hobbies, merlins, peregrines, hen harriers and marsh harriers.

WALK DETAILS

Start/finish: Rame Head Car Park, Torpoint, PL10 1LH

Distance: 2.1 miles (3.4km)

Difficulty: 3/5

Public transport: Regular ferries from Plymouth to Cawsand, about a 1-mile (1.6km) walk from the start

DIRECTIONS

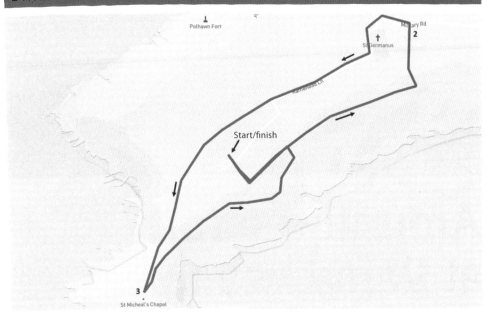

1. Leave the car park by the main entrance and cross the road, heading straight on towards the coast with a field on your left. At the end of the field, turn left on to the South West Coast Path that runs parallel to the sea with the sea on your right. Follow this path past three large fields until you can turn left on to a minor footpath that crosses to a lane at Rame village.

2. Turn left and follow the lane as it curves around the church to the left. Continue along the lane as it curves right, leaving the church behind you. Where the lane bends sharply to the left, carry straight on and follow a footpath through a field and all the way out to the chapel on Rame Head, climbing the steps to reach the top.

3. After exploring the chapel and headland, retrace your outward route back down the steps but bear right at the bottom, following the South West Coast Path back to the car park.

THINGS TO SEE AND DO NEARBY

The Rame Peninsula is sometimes called Cornwall's forgotten corner, and there's no better place to escape the summer crowds. **Whitsand Bay** is a spectacular 3-mile (4.8km) stretch of sand between Rame Head and Portwrinkle, perfect for sandcastling and rock pooling.

05

A marine safari at Wembury

NEAR PLYMOUTH, DEVON

Beach days are great for engaging children in exploring, learning and getting creative outdoors, and coastal walks are filled with interesting things to look at as you go. The South West Coast Path edges the South West of England for 630 miles (1,015km) between Poole in Dorset and Minehead in Somerset, providing countless incredible stretches for walking and exploring.

Just along the Devon coast east of Plymouth, the village of Wembury boasts a reputation as one of the best rock pooling destinations in the country. The rocky coves, slate reefs and vast wave-cut platforms here make it an ideal location for all sorts of marine wildlife, and it is designated as both a Marine Conservation Area and a Special Area of Conservation. Managed by the Devon Wildlife Trust, the Marine Centre at Wembury is a great source of information and provides spotting sheets to help you identify the inhabitants of the local rock pools.

This walk follows the coast path from Wembury Beach to Wembury Point, passing a couple of lovely little beaches along the way – ideal if you're bringing a dog over the summer months when there's a dog ban on the main beach. Look beyond the distinctive wedge-shaped Great Mewstone to the vast blue stretch of sea to spot vessels of all shapes and sizes – from ferries and fishing boats to warships and oil tankers – coming and going at Plymouth.

WALK DETAILS

Start/finish: Wembury National Trust Car Park, Wembury, Plymouth, PL9 0HR

Distance: 2.5 miles (4km)

Difficulty: 2/5

Public transport: Regular buses from Plymouth

DIRECTIONS

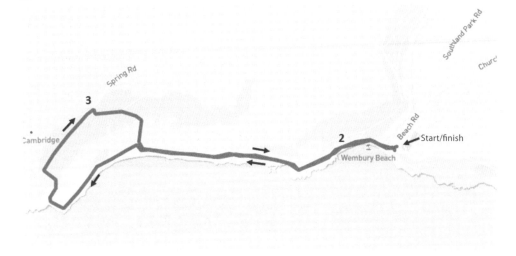

1. From the car park, follow the path downhill to reach Wembury Beach, passing the cheerful Old Mill Cafe on your left. Turn right, following the signposted South West Coast Path westwards along the coast with the sea on your left.

2. Continue following the coast path until you reach the headland at Wembury Point, looking out to the Great Mewstone. Admire the views, then turn right, leaving the coast path and heading up the hill, away from the sea. Bear right on the main path and follow this along the top of the headland until you reach the surfaced road at Marine Drive.

3. At the small parking area, turn right and follow a footpath downhill, through trees, to reach the South West Coast Path. Turn left and follow your outward route back to Wembury Beach.

THINGS TO SEE AND DO NEARBY

There's lots to explore along the coast path in either direction from Wembury. Over the summer months from **Warren Point**, 1 mile (1.6km) or so to the east of the beach, you can hop on a passenger ferry to the pretty twin villages of **Newton Ferrers** and **Noss Mayo**, which are joined by a tidal causeway. Further west, the **Hoe at Plymouth** offers enjoyable walking around the iconic red-and-white-striped lighthouse.

Explore a medieval village on Dartmoor

HOUND TOR, DEVON

Whether they're walking or learning, kids love an inspiring and achievable goal, and summits don't come much more enticing than the rocky granite stacks of Hound Tor, viewed from the start of this walk. A wide, grassy path leads straight up to the rocks, inviting enough that even younger children will often happily run all the way. Once you're there, you'll find endless nooks and crannies to explore and, for the more adventurous, clambering to the very top brings the reward of panoramic moorland views.

Legend has it that Hound Tor's distinctive shape is the mighty hunter, Bowerman, and his pack of fearsome hounds, turned to stone by a coven of disgruntled witches. Bowerman's Nose, a distinctive rocky outcrop that resembles a face, stands at Hayne Down, about 1 mile (1.6km) away.

Continuing over the top of the hill from Hound Tor brings you to the peaceful and atmospheric remains of a settlement of 13th-century traditional Devon longhouses. These would once have housed a family at one end and livestock at the other, and you can still pick out small but recognisable details as you wander around. The land here was first farmed in the Bronze Age and the village is thought to have been abandoned in the early 15th century.

WALK DETAILS

Start/finish: Swallerton Gate Car Park, near Hound Tor on the B3387, Manaton, TQ13 9XG

Distance: 1.4 miles (2.3km)

Difficulty: 2/5

Public transport: Sporadic buses to Swallerton Gate including the Haytor Hoppa from Newton Abbot train station – summer service only

DIRECTIONS

1 From the car park, cross the road and head in a south-easterly direction up the grassy moorland towards the obvious rocky summit of Hound Tor. Head straight through the middle of the main stacks and continue in the same direction down the hill on the other side.

2 Carry straight on down the hill until you reach the medieval village with its stone-walled enclosures. This is a fascinating place to explore and a wonderfully peaceful spot for a picnic.

3 For the return walk, leave the medieval village and head straight for Greator Rocks – the long rocky ridge just to the south of the settlement. Turn right as you reach the Rocks and follow the path along its base. Follow this path back up the hill towards Hound Tor, passing to the left of the Tor as you reach it and picking any of the obvious paths back down to the road and car park.

Map labels: Start/finish · The Hound of the Basket Meals · Hound Tor · Quarry · Cairn and Kist · Hound Tor Deserted Medieval Village · Greator Rocks

THINGS TO SEE AND DO NEARBY

The imposing rocks at **Haytor** are only a couple of miles from Hound Tor and the ascent to the top is another deservedly popular walk for families of all ages. The loop from Hound Tor to Haytor and back is about 4 miles (6.4km) and is suitable for older children. There are some superb paddling spots and a rope swing at **Becka Brook**, but this route does require a map and some navigation, particularly in poor weather.

The National Trust's **Parke** estate lies on the eastern edge of Dartmoor, just outside the small town of Bovey Tracey. Free to access, the estate rambles around the River Bovey, with a selection of waymarked walks of different distances to suit everyone. There's an excellent child-friendly cafe and regular family-focused events, from Apple Day to Parkrun.

Around the rocks at Baggy Point

CROYDE, NORTH DEVON

The great rocky slabs that edge the coast at North Devon's Baggy Point are popular with rock climbers and you can often spot them making their way up the faces from the safety of the well-maintained trails that loop the headland. This walk starts just above the beautiful sandy beach at Croyde, another superb sporting venue, prized for its excellent surf. From Croyde, there's a winding path along the rugged coastline, which eventually brings you to Baggy Point. A little further on, there's a trig point to discover, along with glorious views in all directions.

The return trip takes you inland, crossing fields before dropping back to the pretty National Trust tea room at Croyde, or you can take the path parallel to the outward walk for a slightly shorter and less hilly option. The sheltered sandy beach makes a relaxing afternoon playground, particularly out of season when it's incredibly peaceful. It's also a perfect spot for watching the many seabirds that make their homes in this special place.

As well as its exhilarating rock climbing, Baggy Point is also famous for its fascinating geology, in particular the local Devonian sandstone, formed between 417 and 354 million years ago. This stretch of coast is a great place to find 'erratics' – large boulders deposited by glaciers, often from hundreds of miles away. One of the best-known is a 12-ton pink granite boulder on nearby Saunton Sands, thought to have been transported here by glacier from western Scotland.

WALK DETAILS

Start/finish: Baggy Point National Trust Car Park, Croyde, EX33 1PA

Distance: 2.5 miles (4km)

Difficulty: 2/5

Public transport: Regular buses from Barnstaple, where there is a train station

DIRECTIONS

1. Leave the car park and turn right on to the lane, following the signpost that reads 'Baggy Point 1 mile'. Stay left where the path forks, following the coast path. Shortly after you pass a driveway to a large house on your right, keep an eye out for some whale bones to the right of the path – the remains of a whale that washed up on Croyde Beach in 1915.

2. Continue along this path until you reach the headland, passing a memorial to Henry Williamson, author of the novel *Tarka the Otter*. At the headland, there are great views along the coast and also of the rocks at Baggy Point. Outside of bird-nesting season, you'll often spot climbers scaling the vast slabs here.

3. Follow the path as it takes a sharp right and goes through a gate to reach an old coastguard lookout point. Caution: keep away from the cliff edges here, particularly with dogs and children. Just after

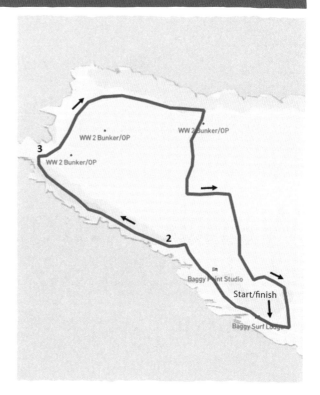

another gate there is a path to the right, signed 'NT car park ¾ mile'. Follow this path across the headland, crossing a couple of stiles, back to the car park and the National Trust tea room at Croyde.

THINGS TO SEE AND DO NEARBY

The Tarka Trail is a 180-mile (290km) walking and cycling route around beautiful North Devon, 30 miles (48km) of which are traffic free. A quiet country lane joins Croyde to the Tarka Trail, making a lovely family cycle ride.

If you'd prefer to explore the sea, there are several surf schools nearby and **Croyde** is well regarded for its surf.

Wander through time at the Valley of Rocks

LYNMOUTH, EXMOOR

The Valley of Rocks, on Exmoor's rugged coast, is a dry valley that once channelled the East Lyn River off the high moor into the Bristol Channel. This peaceful place, surrounded by otherworldly rock formations and edged by a rugged stretch of coastline, has inspired many over the years, including the English Romantic poets Wordsworth and Coleridge. The valley's rocks are exposed Devonian Lynton beds, which are geologically fascinating and abundant in fossils. You'll often spot the local feral goat population balancing improbably on the outcrops.

This walk begins at the heart of the valley, heading straight for one of the most dramatic sections of the 630-mile (1,014km) South West Coast Path, an ever-present guide around this part of England. Running at half height between the towering rocks and the thundering sea, this stretch is a real spectacle and exhilarating to walk along. Caution: although the path is wide and well surfaced, keep younger children and dogs close by. There's a good climb at the halfway point that reaches the higher headland and provides some outstanding moorland and coastal views before you drop back into the valley to finish.

WALK DETAILS

Start/finish: Valley of Rocks Car Park, Lynton, EX35 6JH

Distance: 3.3 miles (5.3km)

Difficulty: 3/5

Public transport: Regular buses from Barnstaple, where there is a train station, to Lynton

SOUTH WEST ENGLAND

DIRECTIONS

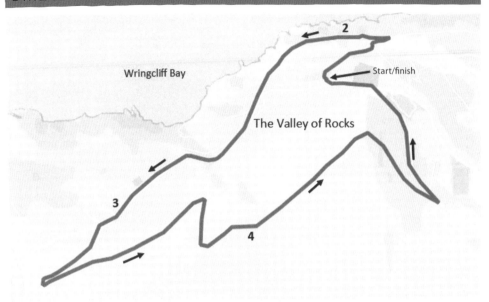

Wringcliff Bay

Start/finish

The Valley of Rocks

1. From the car park, cross the road and follow the footpath with Hollerday Hill to your right. Bear left at the path junction and drop down to reach the South West Coast Path. Turn left on to this and follow it with the sea on your right.

2. Follow the coast path past the towering structure of Castle Rock on your right. At Castle Rock, you can drop down to the beach at Wringcliff Bay for some further exploring should you wish. Otherwise, continue straight on until you reach Lee Abbey on your right.

3. Turn left, leaving the coast path and following the zigzag path up the hill towards Six Acre Wood. Take the sharp left at the woodland and then bear left at the next junction to follow a minor path through the heather and along the top of South Cleeve, with the sea on your left.

4. Follow this path as it runs above the valley, wending right and then left before descending back to the car park to finish.

THINGS TO SEE AND DO NEARBY

Take a ride on the **water-powered cliff railway** that connects **Lynmouth** and **Lynton** – 500 vertical feet (140 metres) apart. The walk can also be started at Lynton train station, close to the town's many amenities.

Climb to the summit of Exmoor

DUNKERY BEACON, SOMERSET

Rising to 1,703 feet (519 metres) above sea level, Dunkery Beacon is the highest point in both Exmoor National Park and the county of Somerset. This part of Exmoor is rich in history, with Bronze Age burial sites, two Iron Age hill forts and a deserted medieval settlement – perfect for the whole family to explore on this engaging walk. There's plenty of wildlife to spot here, too, and Dunkery and its surrounding woodland is a Nature Reserve, conservation area and Site of Special Scientific Interest. Keep watch for majestic red deer and shaggy Exmoor ponies grazing, kestrels and skylarks soaring overhead, and a fascinating mixture of mosses, lichens, ferns and deciduous trees dotted around the heather-clad moorland.

This route follows the inviting main path straight to the top of Dunkery Beacon from the car park, meaning that it's ideal for mini mountaineers who like to have the summit in sight right from the start. The impressive cairn at the top is a great goal, too – a good scramble for those who enjoy heights. Take in the fantastic views out across Exmoor's purple heather-clad moorland to the rolling green countryside beyond, and across the Bristol Channel to Wales.

WALK DETAILS

Start/finish: Dunkery Gate Car Park, Dunkery Beacon, TA24 7AT; grid ref SS895406

Distance: 3 miles (4.8km)

Difficulty: 3/5

Public transport: Nearest bus calls at Wheddon Cross, 2 miles (3.2km) away

DIRECTIONS

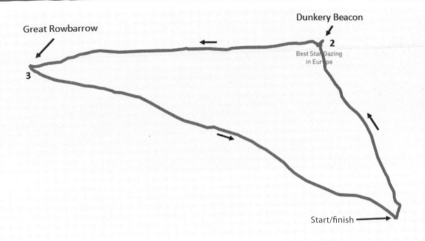

1. From the car park, cross the road and follow the obvious path up the hill in a north-westerly direction to the summit of Dunkery Beacon. Here, a large stone cairn commemorates the transfer of ownership from private estates to the National Trust in the 1930s. It's a good spot at which to pause and take in the views across the surrounding moorland and over the Bristol Channel to Wales.

2. Smaller children may prefer to simply turn around here and freewheel all the way back down to the start. Alternatively, to complete the full walk, turn left, leaving the summit and following the obvious path. Bear right at the fork to continue west along the ridge, slightly downhill at first and then climbing past Little Rowbarrow to reach a path junction and cairn just south of Great Rowbarrow.

3. Turn sharp left and head south-east downhill, crossing the Macmillan Way West – a waymarked trail that runs for 102 miles (164km) from Castle Cary in Somerset to Barnstaple in North Devon – before descending to the road at Dunkery Bridge to finish.

THINGS TO SEE AND DO NEARBY

The nearby stretch of coast north of Exmoor has lots on offer for families, including **Dunster Castle** (National Trust), the **West Somerset steam railway** and **Selworthy Beacon**, another great mini hill with beautiful coastal and moorland views on the **Holnicote Estate**. The **Periwinkle Tea Rooms** in picturesque Selworthy village is renowned for its cream teas.

Poetry and geology at Kilve
QUANTOCKS, SOMERSET

Kilve sits at the northern tip of the Quantock Hills on a rocky stretch of coastline with views across Bridgwater Bay to Wales. These beautiful surroundings inspired the poets and friends, William Wordsworth and Samuel Taylor Coleridge to write several well-known works including Coleridge's longest poem, *The Rime of the Ancient Mariner*. In fact, these regular visitors were at one time suspected of being French spies, rather than poets simply taking in the view and establishing the English Romantic literary movement.

Kilve is also popular with geologists for its unusual rock types and formations. Take a look at the giant folds of rock and imagine the huge forces that helped create them. The cliffs here are Blue Lias – layers of limestone, mudstone and shale, deposited during the early Jurassic about 200 million years ago. The oil-rich shales were once explored as a potential source of oil and the retort house at Kilve Beach Car Park is a remnant of a 1924 drilling, although no significant findings were made.

The Bristol Channel has one of the largest tidal ranges in the world – second only to Canada's Bay of Fundy – reaching 39 feet (12 metres) in the Kilve area, so expect considerable tidal variation depending on when you visit. Low tide is the perfect time to explore the numerous lines of rock pools and also to look for fossils – it's a particularly good place in which to find ammonites.

WALK DETAILS

Start/finish: Kilve Beach Car Park, Bridgwater, TA5 1EG

Distance: 3 miles (4.8km)

Difficulty: 2/5

Public transport: Buses 14 and 15 from Bridgwater to Minehead. Trains to Bridgwater.

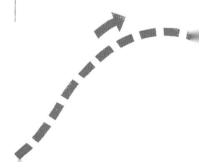

DIRECTIONS

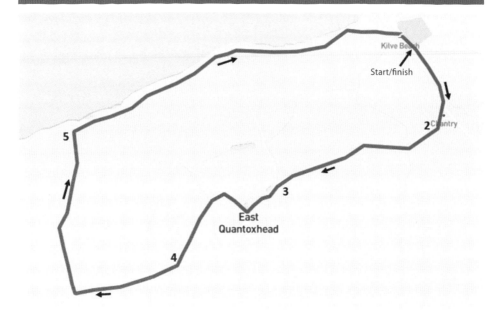

1. From the car park, walk back up the lane to the ruined chantry, turning right through the gate and into the churchyard. Pass to the left of the church and go through a kissing gate into a field.

2. Follow the track across the field, bearing right to go through a gate and skirting the northern edge of East Wood. A stile into the wood permits access over the spring and summer months. Otherwise, keep straight ahead and follow the track across a stream to reach a lane.

3. Turn right on to the lane, then left just before the Tudor Court House, into a car park. Cross this and go through a kissing gate into a field. The path bears right to St Mary's Church, which you can visit. Otherwise, bear left to reach a gate, going through and crossing a field to reach a lane. Turn right on to the lane.

4. Where the lane bends left, stay straight ahead on to a grassy track. Follow this to the top, then turn right on to a signed permissive path. Follow this alongside fields to reach the coast.

5. Turn right here and follow the coast path back to the start.

THINGS TO SEE AND DO NEARBY

Visit the **Chantry Tea Gardens** for a cream tea.

The **Quantock Hills** are great to explore – cycle along the bridleway that traverses the main ridge or climb to the top of **Wills Neck** (Walk 11), the highest point on the hills, for a trig point and panoramic views.

Make a wish on the Quantock Hills

WIVELISCOMBE, SOMERSET

The Quantock Hills stretch for about 15 miles (24km) from the Vale of Taunton Dean in a north-westerly direction to Kilve and West Quantoxhead on the Bristol Channel coast. England's first Area of Outstanding Natural Beauty (AONB), as designated in 1951, the Quantocks offer many excellent opportunities for exploration and adventure. The area boasts a rich diversity of flora and fauna, from the many trees that cloak the sloping hillsides to sweeping heathland. Look out for birds such as skylarks, meadow pipits, redpolls, jays and yellowhammers.

This walk follows the medieval Drove Road along the Great Ridge and climbs to Wills Neck, the highest point (1,266 feet/386 metres) of the Quantocks. The name for this glorious viewpoint is derived from the Saxon for 'foreigner' or 'stranger'. On a clear day, from the trig point-topped summit, you can see Glastonbury Tor and the Mendips in the east; Hinkley Point nuclear power station and across the Bristol Channel to the Gower Peninsula to the north; the Brendon Hills and Exmoor to the west; and the Blackdown Hills to the south.

The marker stone at the start point is thought to date from the Bronze Age and marks a meeting place on the old drovers' road that ran over the Quantocks from Watchet, Somerset, to Lyme Regis, Dorset. Legend has it, if you sit on the stone you will be granted a wish.

WALK DETAILS

Start/finish: Triscombe Stone Car Park, Taunton Road, Wiveliscombe, Taunton, TA4 4AP

Distance: 2 miles (3.2km)

Difficulty: 3/5

Public transport: Nearest bus stop is Crowcombe village, a 1.5-mile (2.4km) uphill walk to the start

SOUTH WEST ENGLAND

DIRECTIONS

1. From the car park, head south through the gate towards Wills Neck. Bear left after the gate, following a bridleway along the edge of woodland, with the trees on your left.

2. Bear right at the path junction, following another bridleway uphill, gradually curving around to the right to gain the main ridge. Turn right at the next path junction, on to the Macmillan Way West, and follow this straight up the hill to the trig point at the top of Wills Neck.

3. From the summit, continue in the same direction, heading towards Triscombe quarry (disused). Bear right after a short distance, following the obvious path to the right of the quarry and back down to the car park.

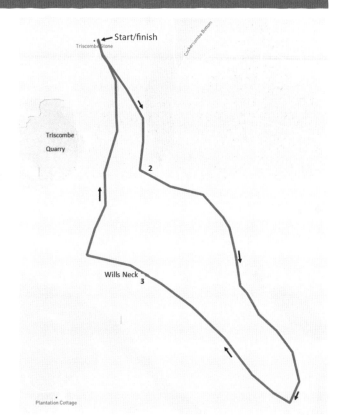

Start/finish

Triscombe Stone

Coomarcombe Bottom

Triscombe
Quarry

2

Wills Neck 3

Plantation Cottage

THINGS TO SEE AND DO NEARBY

The Quantock Hills have an outstanding network of bridleways, which are perfect for mountain biking. The easiest routes follow the Great Ridge along the top but there are countless options to drop down on fun, winding singletrack. Please note: cycling is not permitted on Wills Neck – check the OS Explorer 140 (1:25,000-scale) map for bridleways.

Kilve, to the north of the Quantocks, is a fascinating beach with many rock pools to discover.

12

Conquer the fort at Brean Down

BREAN, SOMERSET

The natural promontory of Brean Down stretches 1.5 miles (2.4km) into the Bristol Channel from the Somerset coast, stands over 300 feet (92 metres) high and is edged by sheer cliffs. Its position has made it an important part of human history, with evidence of settlements dating back to the Stone Age. On the southern side of the Down you can see the remains of ancient field systems and a Roman temple, while on its eastern side there are the banks and ditches of an Iron Age hill fort. Findings from even further back in time include the fossils of mammoths and woolly rhinos that would once have roamed this rugged place.

The vast ruined fort on Brean is one of a series of Palmerston Forts across Britain, built to defend against a possible Napoleonic invasion. It's fascinating to explore these and imagine what they must once have been like. In the Second World War, the area was used for bomber plane and shooting practice, and the gun emplacements are still visible today.

With its military times behind it, Brean Down is now a peaceful, atmospheric place, its limestone landscape rich in wildlife. Listen for the distinctive clink of stonechats, the babble of skylarks from high overhead and ravens cawing. Look out for the white flowers of the rare white rock rose and butterflies, including common and chalkhill blues and marbled whites in summer, and see if you can spot the resident goats, part of a conservation grazing programme. If you're lucky, you might even spot a peregrine falcon hunting at high speed.

WALK DETAILS

Start/finish: National Trust Cove Cafe, Brean, Burnham-on-Sea, TA8 2RS

Distance: 3 miles (4.8km)

Difficulty: 3/5

Public transport: Highbridge train station is 8.5 miles (13.7km) away. From here, take the 112 bus.

DIRECTIONS

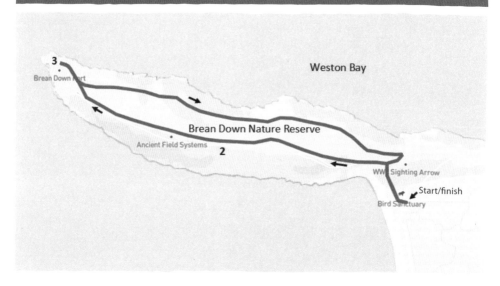

1. Follow the road from the cafe towards the headland, climbing a long flight of fairly steep steps up on to the Down. Take the path to the left, following the southern edge of the promontory until you reach the site of a Romano-Celtic temple, built in around 340CE.

2. Continue along the path towards the main fort, built in 1862 to protect Bristol and Cardiff against the threat of invasion from France. The fort is free to enter and fun to explore.

3. From the fort, walk back along the other side of the Down, passing the banks and ditches marking the site of an Iron Age hill fort. Continue on the path, following it around to the right. This will take you back down the steps to finish at the cafe.

THINGS TO SEE AND DO NEARBY

With their inviting summits and wildlife-rich grasslands, the **Mendip Hills** boast many fantastic, family-friendly walks. Nearby **Brent Knoll** (also National Trust) and **Crook Peak** are both excellent mini mountain walks.

A Jurassic jaunt over Golden Cap

MORCOMBELAKE, DORSET

The airy summit of Golden Cap is the highest point on the south coast of England at 627 feet (191 metres). When seen from out at sea or further along the coast, it rises like a mini Matterhorn, its triangular golden summit formed from local greensand rock. To either side stretches the Jurassic Coast, which runs for about 96 miles (155km) between Studland Bay in Dorset and Exmouth in East Devon. A UNESCO World Heritage Site, its exposed cliffs tell the story of 185 million years of the Earth's past. In the Golden Cap area, the rock is Blue Lias clay, capped with sandstone. Landslides regularly unearth fossils and this is a site of many important finds, including, during the 19th century, that by an 11-year-old girl of the first fossil of an ichthyosaur skeleton.

This walk begins through Langdon Wood, on a circular multi-user trail scented with Corsican pines, carpeted with bluebells in spring and ablaze with beech leaves in autumn. It's a good place to see blue butterflies in summer, while breaks in the trees offer surprise views over the rolling west Dorset countryside. Emerging from the trees, there's the steep ascent to the summit of Golden Cap to tackle, for which you'll be rewarded with outstanding coastal views from the wide, flat summit plateau. The descent takes you around the base of the hill, past St Gabriel's Wood and the ruins of Stanton St Gabriel church, and finishes back through the woodland where there's a wild play area for those with energy left to burn.

WALK DETAILS

Start/finish: Langdon Hill National Trust Car Park, Morcombelake, DT6 6EP

Distance: 2.8 miles (4.5km)

Difficulty: 4/5

Public transport: Nearest train station is Axminster, 7 miles (11.3km) away. Coastline X53 and First 31 bus services run through Morecombelake – alight next to Moore's Biscuits factory and walk along the footpath behind the factory following signs to Langdon Hill.

SOUTH WEST ENGLAND

43

DIRECTIONS

1 From the car park, go through the gate signed to Golden Cap, turning right onto the main path. Follow this path as it curves around Langdon Hill, running through beautiful mixed woodland.

2 Turn right off the main path, leaving the woods and continuing to follow signs for Golden Cap. Stay left and follow the most direct path to the summit, with several stepped sections along the way. The summit plateau is exciting to explore, with a trig point and incredible views along the Jurassic Coast towards Portland in the east and Lyme Regis and East Devon in the west.

3 Leave the summit of Golden Cap at the opposite end to where you arrived, following the South West Coast Path as it zigzags down the hillside. Cross the field boundary at the bottom of the main slope, bearing right and heading across the field to St Gabriel's. The ruins of a medieval chapel stand on a former Saxon settlement in this peaceful part of the estate – you can stay in the National Trust's holiday cottages, formerly an 18th-century manor house.

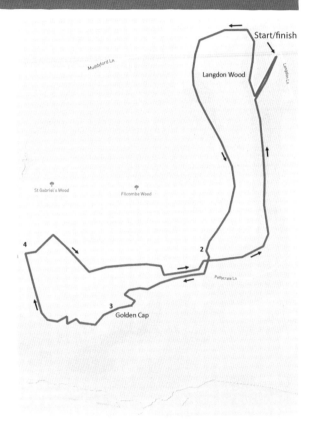

4 Turn right on to the path at St Gabriel's and follow this around the base of Golden Cap to rejoin your outward path emerging from Langdon Wood. Turn right on to the main circular path around Langdon Hill and follow this back to the car park.

THINGS TO SEE AND DO NEARBY

The National Trust-owned **Golden Cap** estate covers 2,000 acres of coast and rolling countryside. There's a shop, cafe and visitor centre, and the estate is free to enter.

For an alternative walk, **Seatown**, at the eastern foot of Golden Cap, is a great place to start an out-and-back ascent of the hill, complete with a good family-friendly pub, The Anchor, and campsite.

The hidden trails at Corfe Castle

CORFE CASTLE, DORSET

The fairy tale ruins of Corfe Castle stand on the top of a long ridgeline, guarding the principal route across the Purbeck Hills. The castle was built in the early 12th century for King Henry I, son of William the Conqueror, on the site of an earlier castle, and withstood the English Civil War as a Royalist stronghold. It was besieged twice – in 1643 and again in 1646 – only to be destroyed on Parliamentary orders. The sight of the ruins of the towering keep, reaching skywards from the top of a rounded hill, really captures the imagination. It is said that Corfe was the inspiration for Kirrin Castle in Enid Blyton's Famous Five books.

Surrounding the castle, the Purbeck Hills rise and fall along a ridge of chalk downland between Lulworth Cove in the west and Old Harry Rocks in the east. This sculpted landscape is exciting to explore, with inviting trails running along the tops of the long, grassy ridgelines and hills that are steep but short.

This walk begins on the outskirts of Corfe Castle village, heading across fields to the chalk ridge at the west of the ruin. Skirting the base of the hill, it makes a steep ascent to the top of the ridge, bringing you to a spectacular viewpoint across to the castle.

Start/finish: West Street Car Park, Corfe Castle, Wareham, BH20 5HH

Distance: 1.9 miles (3.1km)

Difficulty: 3/5

Public transport: Wareham train station is 4.5 miles (7.2km) away. Bus service 40, Poole to Swanage, passes Wareham train station and Corfe Castle.

DIRECTIONS

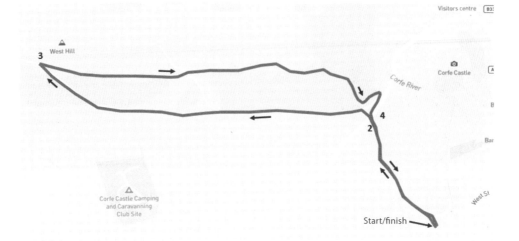

1 From the car park, head north-west, following a footpath across fields away from the village. Stay right at the path junction, continuing north-west across the fields and to the right of some earthworks to reach a road.

2 Cross with care and go straight ahead to meet a wide track, turning left here and following the track along the base of the ridge. Ignore the first turning on the right, but take the next one, following it steeply uphill to reach the top of the ridge.

3 Turn right and follow the path along the top of the ridge, heading for Corfe Castle. On reaching the end of the ridge, either descend steeply down the right-hand corner or retrace your steps to take the less-steep alternative back to the track.

4 From the bottom of the hill, re-cross the road and follow the footpath back across the fields to the car park.

THINGS TO SEE AND DO NEARBY

Less than 6 miles (9km) along the Purbeck Ridge to the east, **Old Harry Rocks** stretch out into the sea, edging the wide sandy arc of **Studland Bay**. This triplet of chalk formations, just off the mainland at **Handfast Point**, marks the easternmost end of the **Jurassic Coast World Heritage Site**, 95 miles (153km) from its western extremity in Exmouth, East Devon. As well as being a wonderful place to spend the day at the beach with a bucket and spade, **Studland** is fantastic for paddling, swimming, kayaking and paddleboarding.

SOUTH WEST ENGLAND

47

15

Hunt for the hill fort in Leigh Woods

BRISTOL, AVON

Lining the western edge of the Avon Gorge, opposite the city of Bristol, the ancient, broadleaved woodland at Leigh Woods was once part of neighbouring Ashton Court Estate. In autumn, it's a blaze of colour, though the area is an uplifting natural oasis to escape to at any time of the year. The northern part of the woods, with its network of waymarked walking and cycling trails, is looked after by Forestry England, while the southern part – a National Nature Reserve – is cared for by the National Trust. More than 300 species of fungi grow on and around the old trees, so look out for them as you go. You'll see plenty of other signs of wildlife, too, including birds, such as the increasingly rare bullfinch, bats and insects.

This walk follows the accessible 1.6-mile (2.6km) purple waymarked trail, leading you on a winding journey through the trees to reach Stokeleigh Camp, an Iron Age promontory hill fort edged by steep banks. Exploring the centre of the fort, you'll discover a hidden wild meadow, and further on, at the eastern edge of the fort, spectacular views open out across the Avon Gorge.

Start/finish: Leigh Woods National Trust Car Park, Abbots Leigh, Bristol, BS8 3QE

Distance: 1.6 miles (2.6km)

Difficulty: 2/5

Public transport: X3 and X4 buses from Bristol

DIRECTIONS

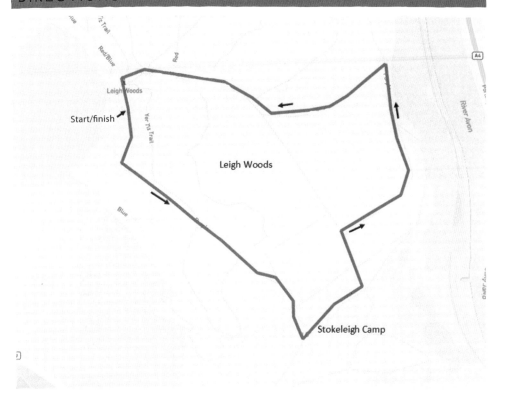

1 Following the waymarked purple trail throughout, this walk takes you from the car park across the parish wall and into National Trust-owned land. It visits Stokeleigh Iron Age promontory hill fort at the halfway point before leading you back to the car park.

THINGS TO SEE AND DO NEARBY

The Leigh Woods Coffee Co trailer can be found in the car park during weekends and school holidays.

Neighbouring **Ashton Court**, with its vast deer park, is also great to explore, or hop on a boat in Bristol and see the city from the river.

16

History and Harry Potter at Lacock

LACOCK, WILTSHIRE

Set amid peaceful Wiltshire countryside and an engaging place for children of all ages at any time of year, National Trust-owned Lacock encompasses three quite different areas. The first, for which it's perhaps best known, is the Abbey, a country house built on a former monastic site. This was once home to William Henry Fox Talbot, the man who is credited with inventing the first photographic negative. Inside, you'll find vaulted cloisters and echoing chambers that starred as various locations in the Harry Potter films, including Professor Snape's classroom. If you're not a National Trust member you'll need to pay to enter the Abbey and gardens. However, Lacock's chocolate-box village, which featured as Budleigh Babberton in the 2009 film *Harry Potter and the Half-Blood Prince*, and the picturesque surrounding countryside are a delight and all completely free to explore.

There are many fantastic walks here, from a simple wander around the village to more adventurous routes. Our choice takes in a bit of both, starting out through the village, crossing the packhorse bridge – an ideal spot for a quick game of Poohsticks – and then heading out to follow the River Avon as it meanders its way back again. There's a short stretch of quiet country lane to finish, where kids and dogs should be kept at heel. The stretch along the river can get muddy at times.

WALK DETAILS

Start/finish: Lacock National Trust Car Park, Hither Way, Lacock, SN15 2LG

Distance: 2 miles (3.2km)

Difficulty: 2/5

Public transport: Bus from Chippenham train station (3 miles/4.8km away)

DIRECTIONS

1. From the car park, cross the road and follow signs to the village, emerging at the entrance to Lacock Abbey. Continue straight on here along High Street, passing the Red Lion pub on your left.

2. Turn right down East Street, passing the Tithe Barn and village hall. At the end of East Street, turn right, then left just before the church to reach the Packhorse Bridge.

3. Cross the bridge, with the weir on your right, and then carry on up the hill, passing allotments on your left. Go through the kissing gate at the top of the hill and follow the obvious diagonal path across the field to reach some houses in the top-right corner.

4. Go through the gate, following a path to reach a lane. Turn right here and right again over the bridge. At the far side of the bridge, look for a stile on your right and cross this into a field. Follow the path alongside the river, with the river on your right, going through a kissing gate and over a footbridge.

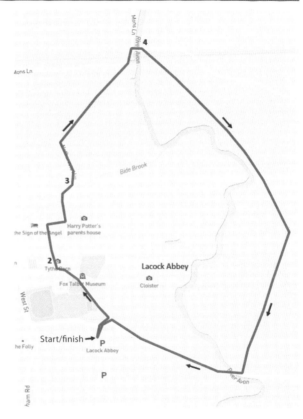

5. Follow the path as it leaves the river and goes left, over a stile and through a field to reach a metal gate. Go through the gate and carry straight on, over a stile and footbridge. Follow the obvious path diagonally across the field to Road Bridge. Cross the bridge and turn right to return to the village.

THINGS TO SEE AND DO NEARBY

Learn about the development of the art of photography at the **Fox Talbot Museum**. Or hop on bikes and explore the nearby **Kennet and Avon canal**, whose peaceful towpath winds into the heart of the city of Bath.

17

Look out for UFOs at Cley Hill

LONGLEAT, WILTSHIRE

Rising from the low-lying fields and farmland on the Wiltshire/Somerset border, Cley Hill's distinctive shape is visible from many miles around. Sculpted by the erosion of ancient seas, prehistoric earthworks and modern quarrying and farming, the ridges, bowls and slopes are all irresistible for young explorers. There are many ways of getting to the top, from the short-but-steep direct route to the one described opposite, which takes you around the flanks of the hill before you ascend via the 'saddle' to emerge at the trig point-topped summit. Whichever route you take, the engaging terrain, inviting paths and 360-degree views from the top make this a great mini mountain for all ages.

Cley Hill is known locally as something of a UFO hotspot, and since the first sightings were recorded in the 1960s there have been many more reported, some with photographic and video 'evidence'. Whether the hill's proximity to the infantry training school at Warminster has anything to do with it or aliens really do visit this quiet corner of Wessex remains to be discovered, but you'll often spot crop circles decorating the surrounding fields.

WALK DETAILS

Start/finish: Corsley, Warminster, BA12 7QU

Distance: 1.4 miles (2.3km)

Difficulty: 3/5

Public transport: Warminster train station is 3 miles (4.8km) away. Bus 53 Warminster to Frome stops nearby.

DIRECTIONS

1 Leave the car park by the main entrance and turn left, following the track towards Cley Hill. Go through the gate at the end and bear right, following the obvious paths around the base of the hill, curving to the left.

2 Bear left and take one of the paths that lead to the top of this side of the hill. Walk straight along the main ridgeline until you reach the summit, marked with a trig point.

3 Descend on any of the paths, choosing one of a steepness you are happy with – they vary greatly! Once back at the base of the hill, make your way back around to the gate and retrace your steps to the car park.

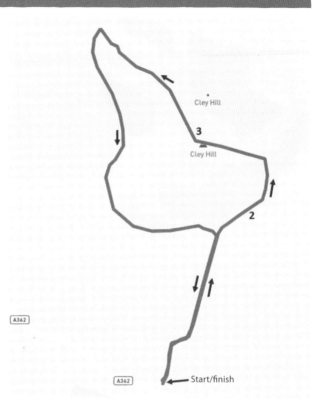

Cley Hill

3
Cley Hill

2

A362

A362 ← Start/finish

THINGS TO SEE AND DO NEARBY

The nearby **Longleat** estate has many enjoyable walks, as well as the popular safari park (paid entry).

Explore the ancient earthworks at **Bratton Camp** and the **Westbury White Horse**, one of thirteen chalk horses etched into the hillsides of Wiltshire.

18

Find a white horse at Milk Hill

ALTON BARNES, WILTSHIRE

At 968 feet (295 metres) above sea level, the summit of Milk Hill is the highest point in the county of Wiltshire. Set atop a sweeping chalk escarpment scattered with fascinating echoes of millennia of human interaction, this is an intriguing landscape and the inviting trails that wind across the sheep-cropped grass call out to kids of all ages. The Alton Barnes white horse is one of 13 white horses carved into the Wiltshire downs' chalk hillsides. Fully re-whitened in 2010, the original horse is a little over 200 years old and is visible from many miles across Pewsey Vale.

This walk starts along the Tan Hill Way, named after the neighbouring Tan Hill, the second-highest point in Wiltshire. Skirting around the northern slopes of Milk Hill you'll join the White Horse Trail, which takes you all the way to the horse, accompanied by glorious views out across the Vale. On the final stretch you'll pass the intriguing earthworks at Adam's Grave, a chambered long barrow dating back more than 4,000 years that would have been part of the numerous Neolithic settlements in this area.

WALK DETAILS

Start/finish: Pewsey Downs Car Park, 1.5 miles (2.4km) north-east of Alton Barnes, nearest postcode SN8 4JX

Distance: 2.7 miles (4.3km)

Difficulty: 2/5

Public transport: Pewsey to Devizes bus stops at Alton Barnes, from where the White Horse Trail links to the walk – adds approximately 1.5 miles (2.4km) of walking

SOUTH WEST ENGLAND

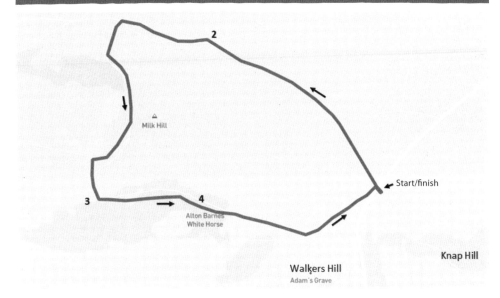

Milk Hill

2

Start/finish

3

4

Alton Barnes
White Horse

Knap Hill

Walkers Hill
Adam's Grave

1 From the car park, cross the road – caution: cars travel fast along this stretch – and follow the path straight ahead, up the hill in a north-westerly direction. This is also the Tan Hill Way. Continue until you reach a junction with a larger track, part of the Wansdyke Path and a medieval ditch.

2 Turn left and follow the track until you can turn left on to the White Horse Trail. Follow this as it contours around the base of Milk Hill. You can detour up to the summit of Milk Hill if you wish to stand on the top of Wiltshire. However, there's no trig point so a bit of guesswork is required to find the highest point.

3 Continue following the White Horse Trail as it curves around to the left, with great views to your right. After an area of scrub, you'll reach the White Horse.

4 From the White Horse, continue following the White Horse Trail as it contours the hillside, curving to the right and then to the left. After crossing Walkers Hill, bear left, leaving the White Horse Trail – which heads right to descend to Alton Barnes – and cross the fields to return to the car park. If you can, detour to explore the fascinating long barrow at Adam's Grave.

THINGS TO SEE AND DO NEARBY

Caen Hill Locks, situated on the Kennet and Avon Canal between Rowde and Devizes, are a flight of 29 locks over a 2-mile (3.2km) stretch of the waterway. They typically take five or six hours to traverse in a boat and are an incredible feat of engineering. There's a small cafe at the locks, along with a wildlife area and newly planted woodland, all of which are ripe for exploring.

SOUTH WEST ENGLAND

19

An ancient oak trail through Savernake Forest

MARLBOROUGH, WILTSHIRE

Savernake Forest is a remnant of a vast, ancient forest that once covered great swathes of Britain. A former royal stag-hunting area, today it is the only privately owned ancient forest in the country, although it is open to the public and managed by Forestry England.

Savernake is thought to be home to the highest concentration of veteran trees in Europe, and many of the great oaks have been named to reflect their unique characters. At 1,000–1,100 years old, and with an impressive girth of 36 feet (11 metres), Big Belly Oak – which stands at the edge of the A346 between Marlborough and Burbage – is one of the oldest trees in Britain, having taken root around the time of the Battle of Hastings in 1066. A designated Site of Special Scientific Interest (SSSI), Savernake is also an important area for wildlife, including, over the summer months, the beautiful and rare purple emperor butterfly.

This figure-of-eight walk follows clear trails around Savernake, visiting seven of the named ancient oaks in the forest. It can easily be shortened to just the smaller of the two loops, or at several other points. It's worth taking a compass with you as, while the directions are straightforward, the forest can be disorientating. Learning to use a compass is also a great way to introduce kids to the art of navigation.

WALK DETAILS

Start/finish: Postern Hill Car Park, Salisbury Hill, Marlborough, SN8 4ND

Distance: 5.5 miles (8.9km) – lots of options for short cuts

Difficulty: 2/5

Public transport: Regular buses from Marlborough – alight at Postern Hill

SOUTH WEST ENGLAND

DIRECTIONS

1 The Bumble Oak stands at the edge of the car park, near to the start. From here, follow the path opposite, which heads into the forest. After 0.5 miles (0.8km), turn left at the crossroads to find the White Road Oak. This ancient tree – with a girth of nearly 23 feet (7 metres) – is well over 500 years old. Carry on down this track, taking the next path on your right, called Long Harry.

2 The path crosses a bridleway, also called Church Walk. Continue straight ahead and, about 110 yards (100 metres) later, take a small grassy path on your left to reach a clearing where you'll find the Saddle Oaks, named after the horizontal growth of their great boughs.

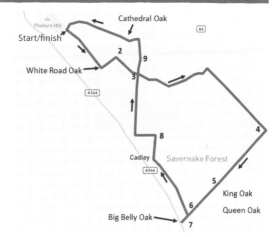

3 Retrace your steps back to the main path and continue straight ahead for about 0.5 miles (0.8km) until you reach Grand Avenue. At 3.9 miles (6.3km) in length, this beech-lined avenue is the longest in Britain and part of the surrounding Capability Brown landscape. Turn right on to the avenue and follow it south-east until you arrive at Eight Walks, a striking meeting point of paths leading away into the forest.

4 The first path on your right – Great Lodge Drive – shortens the walk but misses out several oaks. For the full walk, take the second path on your right, at a right angle to the one you arrived on. After around 0.5 miles (0.8km), shortly after a minor path to your left, take a grassy track on your right. Bear right at the next fork to discover the newly planted Replacement King Oak.

5 Return to the fork and bear left this time, passing the Spider Oak, Original Queen Oak and New Queen Oak. Carry straight on until you reach a crossroads, then turn right and continue until you can take a small path on your right, just before the track meets the main road.

6 Follow the path parallel to the main road for a short distance, looking left for a rough path that heads towards the road, where you'll find the Big Belly Oak. This tree is between 1,000 and 1,100 years old and is supported with a metal girdle around its belly.

7 Retrace your steps and continue following the path, with the main road to your left, until you reach Great Lodge Drive.

8 Turn left and follow the drive for a short distance towards the main road, until you can turn right on to a bridleway, also known as Church Track. Follow this, eventually crossing your outward path near to the Saddle Oaks. Just after this junction you will pass the distinctively shaped Old Paunchy, thought to be about 700 years old.

9 Carry on straight ahead until you reach a track, turning left here and then first right on to a small path. Follow this path through an imposing area of oak and beech until you reach the magnificent Cathedral Oak, thought to be more than 1,000 years old. Continue through the clearing, turning right when you meet a track, to return to the car park.

THINGS TO SEE AND DO NEARBY

Discover more of Wiltshire's fascinating history by exploring the stone monuments of **Avebury** and **Stonehenge** nearby.

At **Crofton Beam Engines**, on the Kennet and Avon Canal on the southern edge of Savernake, you can see the steam engines that once pumped water to this, the highest point on the canal. Open between April and October, under-16s go free and there's also a family-friendly cafe.

SOUTH
EAST
ENGLAND

20

A view of the Needles from Tennyson Down

TENNYSON DOWN, ISLE OF WIGHT

Lying across the Solent from the Hampshire coast, the Isle of Wight is a county in its own right and Britain's second most populous island – the most populous being Portsea in Hampshire, which includes Portsmouth and Southsea and is separated from the rest of the county by the narrow channel of Portsbridge Creek.

This figure-of-eight walk explores the western reaches of the island. It loops the grass- and gorse-covered downland at Tennyson Down – with its prominent monument to a former resident, Alfred, Lord Tennyson – and heads out to the Old Battery, perched high above the iconic Needles.

One of Britain's best-known landmarks, the Needles are the visible remains of a chalk ridge that is thought at one time to have connected the Isle of White to Old Harry Rocks on the Dorset coast, 20 miles (32km) away. Erosion gradually worked its way through the soft chalk, until the Solent River breached the ridge, creating the Isle of Wight. Until 1764, there were four rocks; the fourth – the tallest and most needle-shaped – collapsed during that year's fierce storms.

Perched high above the Needles, the Old Battery is a Victorian fort, built in 1862 and used during both World Wars. It was the site of the world's first radio station, set up by Marconi in 1897 and, in 1898, saw the sending of the first paid wireless telegram – a Marconigram. The National Trust tea room at the Old Battery is a good extension to this walk and a beautiful spot for lunch accompanied by views out to the Needles.

WALK DETAILS

Start/finish: High Down Chalk Pit National Trust Car Park, Totland, nearest postcode PO39 0HY

Distance: 3.4 miles (5.5km)

Difficulty: 3/5

Public transport: Newport to Alum Bay regular bus service

DIRECTIONS

Headon Warren
Barrow
B3322
High Down Inn

Hatherwood Battery
Frenchmans Cove
Start/finish

B3322
The Golf House

Alum Bay

Needles Beacon Replica

4

2

West High Down

Tennyson's Monument

3

High Down
Rocket Test Site

1 Facing the quarry, take the left-hand path out of the car park, then turn right and climb the steps. Continue up a steep path going through a kissing gate to reach the top of the hill and the Tennyson Monument.

2 Turn right and follow any of the paths across the grassy clifftop, aiming for the radio mast in the distance. Once you reach it, go to the right of the mast, dropping down to a road and the coastguard station. You can detour down to the Needles Viewpoint and Old Battery (National Trust members/ paid entry) from here, otherwise follow the road with care around to the right, heading for Alum Bay.

3 Continue along the road until the sharp left-hand corner. Leave the road here, going straight ahead up some steps and through a kissing gate.

4 Follow the path along the lower slopes to the right of the fence and past a farm, then continue along the path as it climbs up the hill to a beacon and gate. Go through the gate and take the rutted path to the left, descending to reach the car park.

THINGS TO SEE AND DO NEARBY

The **Isle of Wight** is a fantastic place for cycling, with an annual cycling festival and more than 200 miles (320km) of cycling routes, including quiet lanes, tracks and bridleways. The 65-mile (100km) waymarked **Round the Island route** is very popular, and can be broken up into sections and ridden over several days. There are plenty of bike hire companies on the island, or bikes can be taken on the ferry.

21

Hunt for history at White Moor and Mallard Wood

LYNDHURST, NEW FOREST

The New Forest is one of the largest areas of unenclosed pastureland, heathland and forest in the south of England. A sanctuary of open space, trees and mixed wildlife habitat within easy reach of some of the South's most populous towns and cities, the area was designated a National Park in 2005. A wealth of fascinating archaeology is scattered through the forest, including 250 round barrows and 150 scheduled ancient monuments.

Numerous footpaths and bridleways lead through mixed woodland, areas of redwood, broadleaf, conifer and heathland cut through by streams and rivers and grazed by New Forest ponies, making this a spectacular place to walk at any time of year. This walk begins at Lyndhurst, in the heart of the National Park, and heads east past Bolton's Bench to the atmospheric open spaces of White Moor. This area has an intriguing military history, the echoes of which can still be seen today through Victorian rifle range butts – banks of earth built up in front of targets – and the remains of trenches dug during the First World War. You'll cross gorse- and heather-clad heath to reach Mallard Wood, winding through old oak and beech trees. In summer you might spot butterflies, such as silver-studded blues and graylings.

WALK DETAILS

Start/finish: Bolton's Bench Car Park, Lyndhurst, SO43 7BQ. Can also be started from Lyndhurst centre

Distance: 3.1 miles (5km)

Difficulty: 2/5

Public transport: Nearest train station is at Ashurst, from where it's a five-minute bus ride to Lyndhurst

SOUTH EAST ENGLAND

DIRECTIONS

1 Leaving Bolton's Bench car park, turn left and follow the tarmac road with the tree-topped hill of Bolton's Bench on your right. Turn left to the village cemetery, passing another car park to your right.

2 At the entrance to the cemetery, turn left and follow the wall around to the right, then bear left along a grassy path to reach an open area with a bench and an old gravel pit. Walk behind the bench, descending to a track junction.

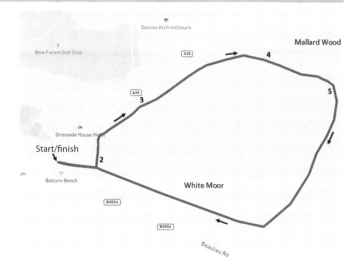

3 Continue straight ahead, following the path alongside a trench that's overgrown with bracken. Go straight across at the next junction at the edge of the woodland. Follow the path around to the left, aiming for a group of Scots pines, then, at the next junction, take the second exit on the right and follow this into Mallard Wood.

4 Follow the path through the wood as it curves to the right, then take the next right fork, emerging on to open heathland. Follow the path diagonally across the heath. Cross a small side stream at the opposite side of the heath, then turn left and walk alongside the Beaulieu River.

5 Reaching another area of open grassland, cross the small footbridge over the Beaulieu River to reach Longwater Lawn. Here, take the old Salt Way, following this away from the river, continuing for about 0.75 miles (1.2km) in the direction of Lyndhurst to reach The Ridge, running parallel to Beaulieu Road. Turn right at the track junction to return to Bolton's Bench.

THINGS TO SEE AND DO NEARBY

In contrast to the New Forest's pony-grazed grasslands and wooded expanses, **Lepe Country Park** on the southern edge of the National Park has a fantastic stretch of coast to explore. The grassy clifftops are a perfect place for a picnic, with views out across the Solent to the Isle of Wight, while the 1 mile (1.6km)-long beach is a great spot for paddling and digging.

22

Butterflies and the Bronze Age at Butser Hill

SOUTH DOWNS, HAMPSHIRE

Covering 1,400 acres across three hills in the South Downs National Park, Queen Elizabeth Country Park is a varied landscape of dense woodland, chalk downland and the highest point on the South Downs Way, Butser Hill at 886 feet (270 metres). Despite its proximity to the busy A3, there's an abundance of wildlife here and the park includes both a Site of Special Scientific Interest and a National Nature Reserve. Walking across the chalk downland over the summer months you can spot up to an incredible 30 different species of butterfly.

This enjoyable walk from the Country Park Visitor Centre takes you up to and around the summit of Butser Hill. It's a good climb to get to the top, but well worth it for the glorious 360-degree views. The hill derives its name from the Old English *Bryttes Ora* meaning 'Briht's slope' and, as you walk, you'll see the marks of millennia of human history etched into the chalk grassland. On the ascent, you'll pass several steeper sections, the remains of a Celtish field system dating back more than 2,000 years. Towards the end of the walk you will pass the remnants of a series of Bronze Age burial mounds created between 3,000 and 4,000 years ago.

WALK DETAILS

Start/finish: Queen Elizabeth Country Park Visitor Centre Car Park, Waterlooville, PO8 0QE

Distance: 3.3 miles (5.3km)

Difficulty: 3/5

Public transport: Bus 37 Havant to Petersfield stops at Queen Elizabeth Country Park

DIRECTIONS

1. From the car park, walk under the A3 road bridge to reach a South Downs Way signpost. Cross the road and follow the path down a short hill between trees and through a gate.

2. Stay right, following the fence line until you reach another gate. Go through the gate and follow the grassy track up the hill, going through the next gate and heading for the radio tower and trig point. This marks the highest point on the South Downs chalk ridge at 886 feet (270 metres). Bear right from the trig point, following a wide, grassy track with views along the chalk ridge of the South Downs stretching ahead to reach the sea. Cross another track and turn left at the T-junction. At the next fork, bear left and then right downhill to a water trough.

3. Turn left here and follow the grassy track west along the edge of the escarpment to a wooden gate. Go through this and head downhill, keeping the high ground to your left and the view across the Western Weald to your right. Bear right at the next fork, taking the narrow path towards a fence with a red marker post. Don't go over the stile here; instead, turn left and follow another narrow path to another red marker post.

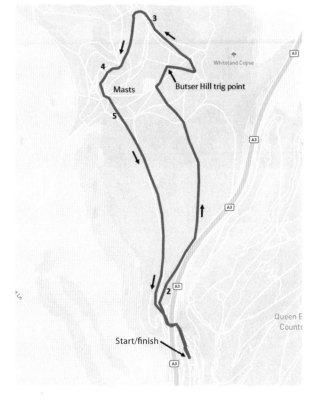

4. Take the rough path uphill just past the end of the burial mounds to reach the next marker post. At the top of the hill, cross the main track and turn left on to a narrow but well-worn trail along the edge of a deep, steep-sided dry valley. Continue until you reach the head of the valley, known locally as Grandfather's Bottom, then bear left at the fork and walk up the hill to reach a gate.

5. Go through the gate and cross a tarmac drive – there are sometimes refreshments available at the conical hut here. Go straight ahead, following a grassy track, first alongside the fence line but then bearing left, aiming for the blue post marking the South Downs Way. Follow the South Downs Way down the hill and back to the visitor centre.

THINGS TO SEE AND DO NEARBY

Nearby **Butser Ancient Farm** is an experimental archaeology site that welcomes visitors throughout the year. It is paid entry but well worth a visit, particularly for budding historians and archaeologists. Here, you'll discover reconstructions of ancient buildings from the Stone Age, Iron Age, Roman and Anglo-Saxon periods, which often feature in films and documentaries. The farm also grows ancient crops and keeps rare breed animals.

23

Meander round the mansion at Greys Court

SOUTH DOWNS, HAMPSHIRE

Just 3 miles (4.8km) from the historic town of Henley-on-Thames, the 16th-century mansion at Greys Court and its manicured gardens stand within a wider estate of classic Chilterns scenery, with beech woodlands, rolling, open countryside and beautiful views. The estate is owned by the National Trust and the lovely grounds – which include a maze, walled garden and wild play area – require membership or payment to enter. The wider grounds, however, contain a network of public footpaths, perfect for exploring on a walk. Spring is a wonderful time to visit, when flowers are blooming in the gardens and bluebells carpet the woods. Listen out for woodpeckers and skylarks and look for the many butterflies that visit the estate.

The accessible route described follows red arrow waymarkers throughout – great fun for children to spot and point out the way – and was a joint project between the National Trust and the Chiltern Society. The footpaths are well marked and maintained so it's easy to extend the walk should you wish to, including to Henley; in fact, you could begin the walk here should you wish to add on a couple of miles.

WALK DETAILS

Start/finish: Greys Court National Trust Car Park or informal parking on Rocky Lane, Henley-on-Thames, RG9 4PG

Distance: 2 miles (3.2km)

Difficulty: 2/5

Public transport: Henley-on-Thames train station is 3 miles (4.8km) away. Take the Chiltern bus from Henley to Rotherfield Greys, a 0.25-mile (0.4km) walk from the start.

SOUTH EAST ENGLAND

DIRECTIONS

1 Go through the gate at the top of the car park, then pass the picnic area and follow the field boundary down the hill. Pass through the gate inscribed 'Johnnie's Gate' – one of several around the estate dedicated to members of the Brunner family who once lived here.

2 Walk alongside the fence until you can turn left through a small gate. Cross the bridge by the pond, then carry on along the edge of the farmyard to reach a lane. Enter the field opposite and walk diagonally across this to the edge of beech woods.

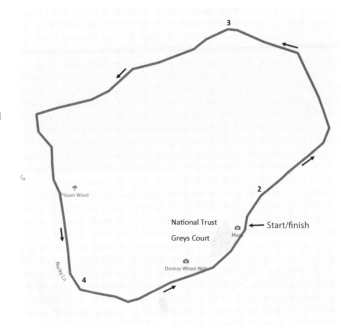

3 Enter the woodland and turn left, following the path through the trees, passing disused clay and flint pits. Continue on the path as it heads downhill, turning left at the bottom into Pissen Wood.

4 Continue until you can turn left on to a footpath just before the gate leading on to Rocky Lane. Follow this on to the house driveway, bearing left to return to the car park.

THINGS TO SEE AND DO NEARBY

Henley is a fun place to visit with kids, with stunning riverside walks, the **Wind in the Willows museum** and **Asquiths teddy bear shop** to start with. Hire a boat and go for a mess-about on the river, or walk up to the impressive weir at **Marsh Lock**, with its long wooden walkway, for a fantastic view of the thundering water.

24

Admire the view from Coombe Hill

CHILTERNS, BUCKINGHAMSHIRE

Coombe Hill stands proud above Aylesbury Vale, topped with the imposing Boer War monument, built in 1904. At 853 feet (260 metres) above sea level, this is the highest viewpoint in the Chilterns and overlooks the Chequers estate, the country retreat of the serving prime minister. The landscape is rare chalk grassland, and is home to more than 40 species of wildflowers and 15 species of butterfly – the reason for its designation as a Site of Special Scientific Interest.

The grassy mounds are anthills, home to the yellow meadow ant, which spends most of its life below ground. The hills can reach a height of 20in (50cm) above ground and extend up to 3.3 feet (1 metre) underground. If they do venture above ground, the ants are generally non-aggressive. However, if they think their nest is under attack they may bite and this can sting. Many species of plant grow in the fertile soil of the anthills. They also have a symbiotic relationship with the Chalkhill blue butterfly, protecting its caterpillars in return for the sugary substance they produce.

In autumn, these woods are brilliantly colourful and fascinating fungi grow in abundance here. You can also enjoy a blustery walk in winter, when the well-maintained trails drain quickly.

The first half, as far as the monument, is accessible for buggies and wheelchairs and makes an excellent out-and-back adventure.

WALK DETAILS

Start/finish: Coombe Hill National Trust Car Park, Lodge Hill, Aylesbury, HP17 0UR

Distance: 1 mile (1.6km)

Difficulty: 2/5

Public transport: Wendover train station is 1.5 miles (2.4km) from the start

DIRECTIONS

1 This route follows orange waymarker posts throughout. From the car park, go through the gate, turn right on to a wide gravel path and follow this past the natural play area on your right. Continue along this gravel track towards the Boer War monument as views open out over the Vale of Aylesbury ahead.

2 From the monument, turn your back on the view and follow the orange waymarker along a path to your right, alongside some bushes. This section follows the Ridgeway National Trail and can get muddy after wet weather.

3 At the fence line at the end of the path, turn left uphill and leave the Ridgeway, following waymarkers weaving through an area of trees and scrub but staying roughly parallel to the fence on your right. On reaching the gate, turn left and then take the next right to rejoin the path back to the car park.

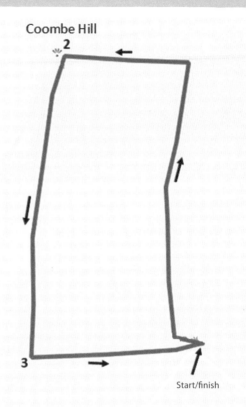

Coombe Hill

Start/finish

THINGS TO SEE AND DO NEARBY

Visit **Buckmoorend Farm Shop** on the **Chequers** estate, where you can sit outside with a hot chocolate or an ice cream, depending on the time of year, or stock up on picnic supplies. The shop is right on the **Ridgeway** and **Icknield Way** National Trails and makes an ideal starting point from which to explore more of the estate.

25

Follow in the footsteps of the Ancients at Ivinghoe Beacon

CHILTERNS, BUCKINGHAMSHIRE

Rising above the Vale of Aylesbury, the Chilterns Area of Outstanding Natural Beauty provides a glorious escape from the bustle of the South East. The region forms part of a system of chalk downs that is more than 65 million years old, running right through England from the Isle of Wight off the south coast to Yorkshire in the north.

An inviting network of trails covers the hills, making them perfect for on-foot exploration. There's a great variety of landscapes to discover, from the long ridgeline of the hills themselves – which rises and falls across the countryside – to woodland, heath, commons and parkland. There are some steeper-sided hills, but in general the terrain is accessible and gently rolling.

Ivinghoe Beacon, a shapely hill that marks the northern tip of the Chiltern ridge, stands within the boundary of the National Trust's Ashridge Estate. It's an inspiring place to visit, with a fascinating history, including Bronze Age earthworks, and rare wildlife – keep an eye out for wild orchids and rare Duke of Burgundy butterflies. The trig pillar-topped summit is the starting point for two National Trails – the Ridgeway and the Icknield Way – both of which follow ancient routes used for millennia by soldiers, herdspeople and travellers.

WALK DETAILS

Start/finish: Ivinghoe Beacon National Trust Car Park, Dunstable, LU6 2EG

Distance: 1.4 miles (2.3km)

Difficulty: 3/5

Public transport: Tring train station is 2 miles (3.2km) away. Buses stop on B489 above Ivinghoe Aston, within 1 mile (1.6km) of the start.

DIRECTIONS

1 From the car park, follow the clear path running parallel to the road with the road on your left, heading towards Ivinghoe Beacon. Where the path meets both the Ridgeway and the Icknield Way at a junction, bear right, following neither of these but instead taking a minor footpath that runs along the foot of the ridge and then climbs to reach the top to the east of the beacon.

2 Turn left at the path junction at the top of the ridge and follow the clear path to the trig point-topped summit of Ivinghoe Beacon. Head south off the top, following the Ridgeway/Icknield Way path down the hill to reach the road at the bottom. Rejoin your outward route here, following the path back alongside the road to return to the car park.

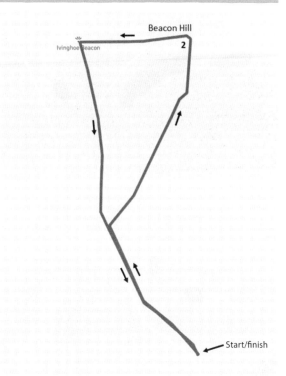

THINGS TO SEE AND DO NEARBY

The wider **Ashridge Estate** is great for exploring, with lots of waymarked trails and a cafe, shop, toilets and visitor centre.

   Whipsnade Zoo is also nearby or, for a quieter adventure, **Whipsnade Tree Cathedral** stands high up on the escarpment, and is a fascinating place to wander around. A peaceful area planted with trees, shrubs and plants, the cathedral was created after the First World War in the spirit of faith, hope and reconciliation and is free to visit.

26

All the way around Frensham Little Pond

FRENSHAM, SURREY

Covering more than 130 acres of wetland, woodland, common and sandy beaches, of which 37 acres is the pond itself, Frensham Little Pond is a haven for a wide variety of birds and other interesting wildlife. It was created in the 13th century on the orders of the Bishop of Winchester, William de Raleigh, who wanted a fish supply for his visits to nearby Farnham Castle. The incoming stream was dammed, and the pond is also fed by springs.

Today, it's a wonderfully peaceful place, and a full circumnavigation of the Little Pond takes you through towering pine trees, past the medieval dam, along an enticing wooden walkway through the reeds and up a short climb to the top of Snowball Ridge. As you walk, watch for terns with their black heads, red legs and acrobatic diving skills. These migratory birds nest on specially designed rafts to keep them safe from predators such as mink. Woodland birds to look and listen for include woodpeckers, nuthatches, jays, small songbirds and even rare nightjars, with their churring call.

The quick-draining trails mean it's a great place to walk at any time of the year and, with a sandy beach and a cafe at the finish, there's something to suit everyone. Further afield at Frensham is the Great Pond, which has a designated swimming area (check in advance for information about blue-green algae, which is often a problem in summer), and the wider commons, networked with trails for exploring.

WALK DETAILS

Start/finish: Frensham National Trust Car Park, Priory Lane, Frensham, GU10 3BT

Distance: 2.5 miles (4km)

Difficulty: 2/5

Public transport: Bus service 19 Aldershot to Haslemere stops at Frensham Common

DIRECTIONS

1 Leave the car park, following signs to the cafe but passing behind the cafe building to reach the pond. Continue along the path as it curves to the right, following the water's edge through woodland and then crossing an area of marsh and reeds on a boardwalk.

2 As you emerge from the woodland, take the path on the right, heading back towards the pond and continuing until you reach a T-junction with a main path.

3 Turn right and follow the main path up to the top of Snowball Ridge, from where there are great views across the common. Turn right at the crossroads at the top and follow the path along the ridgeline through the trees.

4 Carry straight on, following the path as it descends the far end of the ridge, bringing you back to the cafe and beach area by the pond. Follow your outward path from the cafe back to the car park.

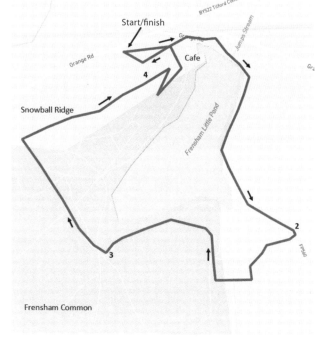

Start/finish
BY522 Titford Common Rd
Grange Rd
Jumps Stream
Cafe
Snowball Ridge
Frensham Little Pond
Frensham Common

THINGS TO SEE AND DO NEARBY

The **Surrey Hills Area of Outstanding Natural Beauty** is a fantastic place in which to escape the busy South East, just a short train ride from central London and with many areas that feel truly wild. **Leith Hill** and **Box Hill** are nearby and make excellent mini mountains to climb, with beautiful views from the summits – and both with a handy cafe, too.

The atmospheric ruins of the 13th-century **Waverley Abbey**, in a peaceful area of grassland by the River Wey, are delightful for children to explore and free to enter. The remains of the vaulted dining hall are particularly breathtaking.

27

Delve the depths of the Devil's Punch Bowl

HINDHEAD, SURREY

The Devil's Punch Bowl is a deep hollow in the heaths and commons of the Surrey Hills, forming a steep-sided nature reserve; a microcosm of flora and fauna. Over the centuries many different stories have grown up around its creation. One claims that the bowl was created by the Devil scooping up handfuls of earth to throw at Thor, god of thunder, in order to annoy him – hence the name of the local village of Thursley. Another suggests it was the result of two arguing giants; one scooped up a huge handful of earth to throw at the other, creating the Punch Bowl, and the clump of earth, missing its target, became the Isle of Wight. The real reason lies in the layered bedrock beneath this part of the Surrey Hills, where an upper layer of sandstone overlies clay. The bowl was created by the action of underground springs, which eroded the sandstone and caused it to collapse.

Until the construction of the Hindhead Tunnel in 2011, the busy A3 London-to-Portsmouth road ran around the south-eastern edge of the Devil's Punch Bowl. The area is now a designated Site of Special Scientific Interest, where extensive work has been undertaken to restore the fragile heathland habitat, leading to the return of rare breeding birds such as woodlarks and nightjars.

This walk follows the Hidden Hindhead Trail, which is signed throughout with clear waymarkers. There are great views from the top of the bowl, and a dip into the heart of the bowl itself.

WALK DETAILS

Start/finish: Devil's Punchbowl National Trust Car Park, London Road, Hindhead, GU26 6AB

Distance: 3 miles (4.8km)

Difficulty: 3/5

Public transport: Regular buses from Farnham and Haslemere, alight at Hindhead

DIRECTIONS

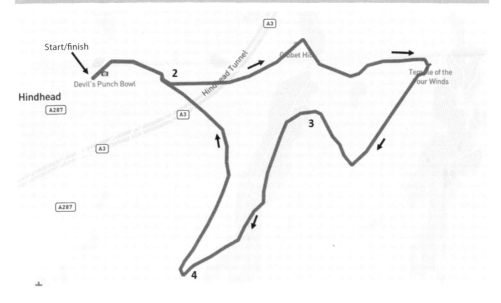

1. From the cafe and car park, follow the signs along the new path towards the old A3 road. Continue along the route, heading north down the surfaced byway and passing the Sailor's Stone.

2. Continue along the former road until you reach a bench and a path leading down steeply to your right. Take this and follow it down the hill and through the trees to reach the plinth of the Temple of the Four Winds. Carry on around the coppice wood, passing a pond on your right then walking up the hill and through a gate.

3. Carry on up the hill until you reach an unmade road. Follow the road downhill until you reach a red-brick house on your left. Turn right through the gate, following waymarkers up a steep hill and past houses on your left to reach a gate.

4. Go through the gate and walk across the heathland, bearing left where the path forks. Continue until you can go through a gate on to the old London road, crossing this to rejoin your outward path back to the cafe.

THINGS TO SEE AND DO NEARBY

Nearby **Waggoners Wells** is a beautiful, peaceful place to explore, with three ponds surrounded by woodland. A cool and shady retreat in summer and ablaze with autumnal colours later on, this is a real oasis in the busy South East.

28

Temples and trig points at Black Down

HASLEMERE, WEST SUSSEX

Hidden within the trees, high on the hillside at Black Down, a lone trig point marks the highest point in the South Downs National Park. Surrounding this wooded summit is a network of inviting paths and trails, edged by fragrant heather and towering pines, with glimpses out across the surrounding heathland and Sussex countryside. The viewpoint at the Temple of the Winds – a favourite spot of Tennyson, who once lived in nearby Aldworth House and built a summerhouse here – is a place that makes even the liveliest of children stop still in awe.

Visit on a warm summer's evening and you'll spot pipistrelle bats bug-catching and you might even hear the distinctive churring call of a shy nightjar. You'll often find gentle Belted Galloway cattle here, too. These are part of a conservation grazing programme to keep invasive plant species down while improving the soil by trampling and fertilising it as they go. Late summer is a great time of year for foraging, when blackberries and bilberries are abundant in the woods and along the tracks.

This walk heads up the main ridge of the hill, taking in a wide loop and visiting the main viewpoints. The trails are easy to follow, but often uneven underfoot.

WALK DETAILS

Start/finish: Tennyson's Lane National Trust Car Park, Haslemere, GU27 3BJ

Distance: 2 miles (3.2km)

Difficulty: 2/5

Public transport: Regular bus and train services to Haslemere, 2 miles (3.2km) from the start

TEMPLE OF
THE WINDS

DIRECTIONS

1 From the car park, take the main track out on to Black Down, following this through the gate and past a noticeboard. Continue up the track, passing a bench and viewpoint on your left.

2 Bear right at the next fork, passing some small ponds on your right and walking through an area of trees until you reach a major track junction called '5 Ways'. Turn left here, heading south out on to the heath.

3 Continue following this main track, passing a viewpoint and crossing the heath, heading south until you come to a crossroads. Turn left here, passing a bench and walking uphill to reach a wooded ridge.

4 Carry straight on at the next crossroads, following signs for the Temple of the Winds. Walk along this path as it descends to this most impressive viewpoint and curved stone seat.

5 Retrace your steps back up the slope, bearing right at the fork and heading north into woodland. Continue on this main path, heading north through the beech hangar. After passing a small pool on your left, take the next right down the sunken path to return to the car park.

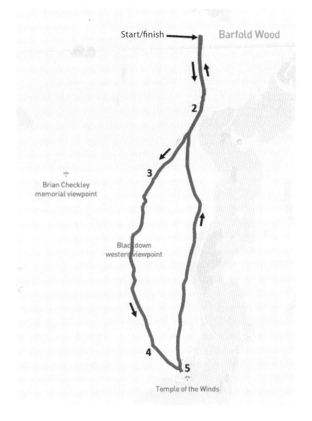

Start/finish ⟶ Barfold Wood

Brian Checkley memorial viewpoint

Black down western viewpoint

Temple of the Winds

THINGS TO SEE AND DO NEARBY

One of the National Trust's beaver reintroduction programmes is taking place at **Valewood** on the **Black Down** estate.

Nearby **Haslemere Educational Museum** boasts a collection of 2,000 flint tools – ranging from axes and maceheads to arrowheads and blades – all of which have been found in the Black Down area. Along with a number of hill forts and other earthworks, these finds document more than 10,000 years of human activity in the area.

29

Hillforts and hurtleberries at Hurtwood and Holmbury Hill

PEASLAKE, SURREY

SOUTH EAST ENGLAND

The Hurtwood, standing high on the greensand ridge in the Surrey Hills, is a magical woodland to wander through and has a fascinating history. Its name was once thought to come from 'hurts', or 'hurtleberries' – the local name for the edible wild blueberries that grow here in abundance – but it may actually derive from the Old English word *ceart* or *churt* for a rough common covered in gorse, broom and bracken.

The area is privately owned, but in 1926 the then owners signed a dedication giving people permission to walk, cycle and ride horses on the land, and this permission is still upheld today. The wood is now looked after by a local charity, the Friends of the Hurtwood. With no statutory funding, the charity relies on supporters and visitors to fund the maintenance and conservation of the woodland. The heather and hurtleberry cover across the woodland floor makes it an ideal habitat for a number of snakes and lizards, including the endangered smooth snake and sand lizards, as well as birds such as the nightjar.

WALK DETAILS

Start/finish: Hurtwood Car Park 1, Peaslake, Dorking, RH5 6NU

Distance: 2.8 miles (4.5km)

Difficulty: 2/5

Public transport: Bus 25 from Guildford, currently schooldays only

This walk takes in a loop through the woodland on clear, well-made trails, and is enjoyable at any time of the year. It passes through the picturesque village of Holmbury St Mary at around halfway, then makes an ascent of Holmbury Hill – an Iron Age hill fort with fantastic views out across the Surrey Hills. On a clear day, you can see the sea at Shoreham to the south, and the London skyline to the north. As the Deed of Dedication pre-dates the Countryside and Rights of Way Act, cyclists and horse riders also use the footpaths at the Hurtwood, so keep an eye out for bikes and horses as you go.

DIRECTIONS

1 From the car park, with your back to the road, walk past the barrier into the woods. With the pond on your right, follow the main path for a short distance, until you can bear left on to a smaller path.

2 Continue straight on at the next two junctions then, just before the path enters a wood, take the sunken path on your right.

3 At the next junction, turn left, following the path past electricity poles until you can turn right through a wooden barrier. Follow the path down a steep bank, crossing a wide path and carrying straight on until you reach a driveway. Go up the driveway, with a house on your right, to reach a lane at Holmbury St Mary. Turn left on to the lane and then right on to a footpath, taking the next right just before the church.

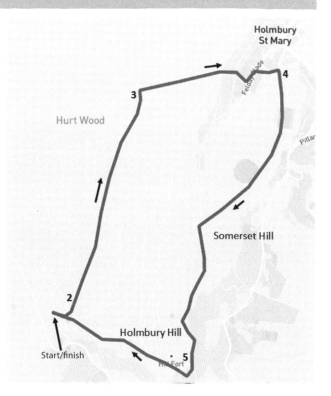

4 Follow this path south, heading uphill through the woods to reach a path junction with the Greensand Way. Keep straight ahead here, joining the Greensand Way (blue GW waymarkers) and following it south all the way to Holmbury Hill, with its intriguing Iron Age earthworks and topograph at the summit.

5 From the summit, with your back to the memorial seat, take the left-hand path (still the Greensand Way) and follow this around the edge of the escarpment, passing a pond on your right and returning to the car park start point.

THINGS TO SEE AND DO NEARBY

To the west of the Hurtwood, the walls of a Romano-Celtic temple are fascinating to explore, with the outer and inner walls clearly marked out in stone. Built between 100 and 400CE, the site was excavated by Victorian antiquarian Martin Tupper, who found a green bronze ring, tiles, pottery and 1,200 coins. Despite more recent excavations, nothing further of interest has been found.

Across the stepping stones at Box Hill

BOX HILL, SURREY

Rising in Surrey's North Downs, less than 20 miles (32km) from London, Box Hill is a popular spot with those looking for fun, challenge and adventure in the great outdoors. On a Sunday morning, the famous zigzag hill is lined with cyclists taking on the hairpin bends, while the hilltop, with its sweeping views, is a great escape from the city. In late spring and early summer the woods at Box Hill are carpeted in delicately scented native wild bluebells. If you look carefully you might spot other wildflowers, too, including dog's mercury, blue violet and lords-and-ladies, along with many different trees such as holly, juniper, hazel, oak, beech and the box trees that give the hill its name.

There's so much for children to do here, from the National Trust's natural play trail to climbing trees and, of course, crossing the famous stepping stones from the Weypole, a 5.9-acre semicircular area between the foot of Box Hill and the River Mole. A ford across the river is thought to have existed at this point since prehistoric times, and the way-pole was a notched post secured in the riverbed, indicating the depth of the water. Stepping stones at this site are first recorded in 1841, although the current stones were installed in 1946, replacing those destroyed during the Second World War as an anti-invasion measure. This delightful walk also passes the Fort, one of Box Hill's oldest buildings.

WALK DETAILS

Start/finish: Box Hill National Trust Car Park, Zig Zag Road, Tadworth, KT20 7LB

Distance: 2 miles (3.2km)

Difficulty: 2/5

Public transport: Box Hill and Westhumble train station is 1.5 miles (2.4km) away

DIRECTIONS

1 Leave the car park and visitor centre, following the surfaced path running parallel to the road, with the view opening out in front of you across the Weald, until you reach the Salomons Memorial.

2 Walk down the sloped path below the Memorial, bearing right and continuing along this path until you reach steps on your left. Follow these downhill through the yew woods – there are 275 steps in total; see if you can count them! Continue on the same path from the bottom of the steps with the River Mole on your left.

3 Where the path forks, bear right, signposted to the stepping stones. When you reach the river you can either cross the stepping stones and turn right, following the far bank, or you can turn right before the stones and follow the near bank.

4 When you reach the footbridge, go through the gate into Burford Meadow. Walk through the meadow until you reach a road bridge in front of you. Take the path just to the left of the bridge, which brings you out on the pavement next to the A24. Turn right here and follow the pavement over the river and past a hotel on your right.

5 Immediately after the hotel, turn right on to a path then, at the fork, bear left uphill on a grassy track. Continue along this uphill as it becomes a wider chalk path. Bear left at the next junction and then right where you join a stony path, carrying on uphill until you reach the building at Box Hill Fort, home to a local population of bats.

6 Continue along the path until you reach the road, turning right here to return to the visitor centre.

THINGS TO SEE AND DO NEARBY

There's a lovely, family-friendly cafe at the visitor centre.

Nearby **Leith Hill** also makes a great walk; the top of its tower, 78 steps up, is the highest point in South East England and is a fantastic place to spot boats on the Channel on a clear day using the telescope.

31

The lighthouse that moved: Birling Gap and Belle Tout

BIRLING GAP, EAST SUSSEX

Birling Gap, part of the Seven Sisters chalk cliffs on the East Sussex coast, is a small National Trust-owned hamlet that's ideally-placed for exploring this fascinating area. Seen from the South Downs Way that runs along the coast, tall, grass-topped chalk cliffs rise and fall like the waves. Inland, a green swathe of ancient downland, rich in wild flora and fauna, gives way in all directions to wide views of Friston Forest and the rolling Sussex countryside.

Nestled between the better-known Beachy Head and Seven Sisters, Birling Gap has a cafe, shop and visitor centre along with a row of former coastguard cottages. Some of the buildings have already been claimed by coastal erosion, which is reducing this stretch of coastline at a rate of up to 3.3 feet (1 metre) a year, while others remain inhabited. The beach at Birling Gap, also a marine nature reserve, is excellent for exploring, with rock pools and areas of pebbles and sand.

This walk begins at Birling Gap and makes an enjoyable loop, starting inland and then heading back along the South Downs Way, including a climb up to the Belle Tout Lighthouse. This fascinating granite structure was the original Beachy Head lighthouse and began operation

WALK DETAILS

Start/finish: Birling Gap National Trust Car Park, Beachy Head Road, Eastbourne, BN20 0AB

Distance: 1.9 miles (3.1km)

Difficulty: 2/5

Public transport: The 13X bus runs hourly from Eastbourne Terminus Road to Brighton via Birling Gap

in 1834 after many wreckings off this part of the south coast. Unfortunately, its position, obscured from ships at sea by the giant cliffs, meant it was not as successful as had been hoped. It was decommissioned in 1902 and a new lighthouse was built at the foot of the cliffs for better visibility. In 1999, to remove the immediate threat of damage by coastal erosion, the Belle Tout was moved 56 feet (17 metres) away from the cliff face to its current position. Caution: please be aware that in places the cliffs are high, unfenced and unstable and therefore children and dogs should be kept away from the edge.

DIRECTIONS

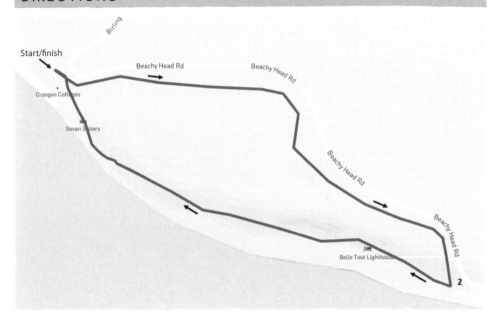

1 From the car park, with the sea on your right and the road on your left, set out on the footpath that runs along the grassy headland, furthest from the cliff edge. Continue to follow this for just under 1 mile (1.6km), until it curves around the right and eventually meets the road.

2 Turn sharp right here and follow the South Downs Way up the hill to Belle Tout Lighthouse. Continue along the South Downs Way all the way back to the car park.

THINGS TO SEE AND DO NEARBY

This section of East Sussex coastline has been inhabited by humans for millennia. The hilltop enclosure of **Belle Tout** is thought to have been the largest prehistoric enclosure in Britain some 5,000 years ago, while the prominent ridge at **Bailey's Hill** features several Bronze Age burial mounds along with evidence of settlement and farming.

Going back even further in time, the beach at **Birling Gap** is a fantastic location for finding fossils.

32

The urban wilds of Epping Forest

EPPING FOREST, ESSEX

Epping Forest was once a royal hunting ground, but today it's the largest public open space in London, covering 6,000 acres and stretching 12 miles (19.3km) from Manor Park in East London to Epping in Essex. Free to enter and open every day of the year, it's owned and managed by the City of London, assisted by groups such as the Epping Forest Conservation Volunteers and the Wren Group. Two-thirds of the forest is designated a Site of Special Scientific Interest, and it is home to more than 50,000 ancient pollard trees – cut low so that their new shoots could feed livestock – and 100 lakes and ponds.

There are many fascinating archaeological sites across the forest, including the intriguing Iron Age hill forts at Loughton Camp in the south, and Ambresbury Banks in the north. Plenty of wildlife makes its home here, including 500 species of rare or endangered insects. Look and listen out for woodpeckers, jays, chiffchaffs and birds of prey circling overhead. Ducks and herons can be seen on the lakes and ponds. You might even spot the herd of rare Longhorn cattle that graze here, upholding the forest's ancient commoners' rights.

Being an urban forest, where the sounds of nature mingle with the roar of the M25 and the whine of planes, it feels very different from many rural woodlands, but the sense of beauty and escape still makes it a special place to be.

WALK DETAILS

Start/finish: Pillow Mounds Car Park, Epping Forest, Waltham Abbey, IG10 4AE

Distance: 2.5 miles (4km)

Difficulty: 2/5

Public transport: Not easily accessible by public transport

SOUTH EAST ENGLAND

DIRECTIONS

1 Pick up the start point from the car park or visitor centre – where there's a cafe, toilets and lots of information on the forest and its wildlife – and follow the Beech Trail arrows throughout. From the start, the route crosses Epping New Road (take care), heading into beautiful beech woods and passing the Lost Pond and Baldwin's Hill pond, both a short detour off the path. From here, it heads to Loughton Camp, which is a perfect place to stop and explore for a while. Finally, it brings you back across the road to the visitor centre.

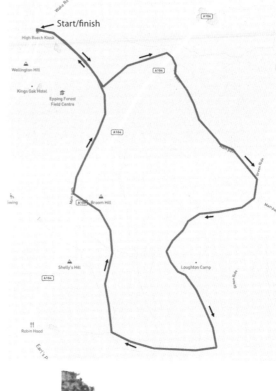

THINGS TO SEE AND DO NEARBY

There are nine waymarked trails in total, each with a different theme and exploring a different part of the forest. Why not try them all?

33

History and hauntings at Ham House

HAM, SOUTH WEST LONDON

The imposing red-brick mansion of Ham House stands grandly on the banks of the River Thames in South West London's Richmond. One of the grandest Stuart houses in the country, it remains much as it would have been at the time of building, and it's a good place to visit in order to learn about life in 17th-century England. There's a hands-on below-stairs room where you can see how bathing was done before hot water was on tap. It is also apparently haunted, with visitors reporting the smell of sweet Virginia tobacco smoke – a favourite of the Duke of Lauderdale, who lived here in the late 1600s – still hanging in the air. Entry to the house and gardens requires National Trust membership or payment.

This part of London is also a wonderful place for walking, easily accessible by train and with a variety of things to see and paths to explore. The Thames Path runs along the front of the house on its 184-mile (296km) journey from the river's source, near Kemble in Gloucestershire, and the Thames Barrier at Charlton, South East London; following it in either direction from Ham House is an enjoyable adventure.

This walk takes in a picturesque stretch of the Thames Path before weaving its way through the peaceful footpaths of Petersham Meadows and past some playing fields before returning alongside Ham House's formal 17th-century gardens.

WALK DETAILS

Start/finish: Ham House, Ham Street, Ham, Richmond-upon-Thames, TW10 7RS

Distance: 2 miles (3.2km)

Difficulty: 1/5

Public transport: Ham House is a 1.5-mile (2.4km) walk on footpaths from Richmond train station

DIRECTIONS

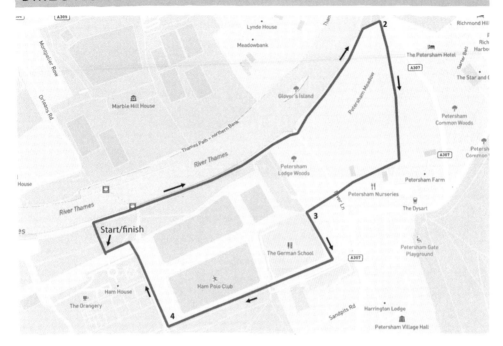

1. Start in front of Ham House, following the path straight towards the Thames. Turn right on to the Thames Path and follow this with the river on your left and grassland and trees to your right. Cross straight over River Lane and continue until the path bears right to meet the A307.

2. Don't go as far as the road; instead, turn right, following a clear path that leads diagonally across Petersham Meadows, going through a gate to emerge on to an unsurfaced road. Turn right and follow this past some houses and tennis courts, crossing straight over River Lane and following the footpath opposite until you reach a junction.

3. Turn left here and follow the path past some school campus buildings. Carry on around the right-hand corner and follow the tree-lined path to reach the back of Ham House gardens.

4. Turn right, following the path with Ham House on your left, turning left once past the House to return to the start.

THINGS TO SEE AND DO NEARBY

Richmond Park is very nearby, and a short extension to the walk can take you over **King Henry's Mound**, a fantastic viewpoint on the edge of the Park.

Eel Pie Island lies in the centre of the Thames, just west of Ham House. Home to a community of artists, this 8-acre island is open for visitors occasionally, with access via a tiny footbridge from the north bank of the river. Catch a ferry from just in front of Ham House and follow the Thames Path to reach it.

The Palladian villa of **Marble Hill House** is also just across this stretch of the water. Owned by English Heritage, it's open to paying visitors.

34

A wild oasis in Richmond Park

RICHMOND, SOUTH WEST LONDON

If you know where to look, there are wonderful, wild places to explore with children all over London. Nearly half of the capital, in fact, is green space. Spring is a perfect time to wander through the city's parks and gardens and there's a wealth of wildlife to spot in the woods and grasslands and on the water – from wildflowers, ducklings and deer to the resident bright-green ring-necked parakeets.

Richmond Park is the largest of London's Royal Parks, covering an area of around 2,500 acres. It is a National Nature Reserve and a conservation area, with an incredible diversity of habitats and, in places, a feeling of wildness that's truly unexpected. It was also the first stronghold of the parakeets that now number in their tens of thousands around London.

There are many tracks and trails around the park and it's a popular place with cyclists, horse riders and on-foot explorers. One of the best for buggies, balance bikes and as a starting point for a further-afield amble is the Tamsin Trail, a 7.35-mile (11.8km) waymarked path that runs around the perimeter and is accessible from any of the main gates. Our choice of walk combines the Tamsin Trail with a section of the Beverley Brook Walk, following the pretty stream edged by pollarded willows. Atmospheric on a misty winter's day or hung with green in summer, this is a great year-round walk where you'll often see the flash of a bright-blue kingfisher skimming across the water and even, in warm weather, deer coming to the brook to drink.

WALK DETAILS

Start/finish: Roehampton Gate Cafe, 142 Priory Lane, Richmond Park, SW15 5JP

Distance: 1.5 miles (2.4km)

Difficulty: 1/5

Public transport: East Putney tube station is less than 2 miles (3.2km) from Roehampton Gate. Bus 337 from East Putney tube station to Stop N, then walk along Priory Lane to Roehampton Gate. Alternatively, walk from Barnes train station.

DIRECTIONS

1 Leaving the cafe, bear left to join the Tamsin Trail for a few hundred yards/metres, until you cross a footbridge over the Beverley Brook. Bear left off the Tamsin Trail here, joining the Beverley Brook Walk, which traces the course of the river.

2 On reaching a footbridge on your left, turn right and cross to the Tamsin Trail, following this back to the cafe.

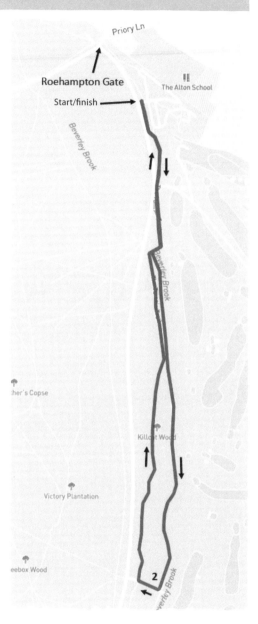

THINGS TO SEE AND DO NEARBY

There are so many other trails and sites to discover in Richmond Park, but one of the most special places is the **Isabella Plantation** – a 40-acre woodland garden set within a Victorian woodland plantation. The collection of azaleas and other shrubs makes this a fascinating place to wander around, and there's a pond and network of streams to explore. The whole area is managed as a Site of Special Scientific Interest. It is run organically and planted with native nectar and berry-bearing plants and trees, and the water features provide habitats for a number of amphibians and invertebrates.

35

Explore the pinetum at Bedgebury

BEDGEBURY, KENT

Bedgebury National Pinetum is home to more than 12,000 trees, making it the largest collection of conifers in the world. It was acquired by the Forestry Commission in 1919 and formalised in 1925, when conifers from London's Kew Gardens were relocated to Bedgebury for its better air quality. Managed by Forestry England, the pinetum has trees from North America, Japan, China, Vietnam and Australasia, and works to help save some of the rarest conifer species on the planet from extinction.

In the great storm of 1987, a third of the trees were sadly lost. Afterwards, a different planting strategy was used, grouping trees aesthetically rather than in species groups and therefore reducing the likelihood of whole species being wiped out in future storms.

This walk follows the waymarked Hidden Secrets trail. The pinetum is a tranquil haven for wildlife, and you might spot signs of wild boar, or see fallow and roe deer grazing peacefully. Look and listen out for woodland birds, such as goldcrests with their shrill 'peep' calls, hawfinches, woodpeckers, siskins, marsh tits and nuthatches – usually seen hanging upside down on the bird feeders near to the visitor centre. Butterflies – such as the rare dark green fritillaries and white admirals – can be seen, along with wildflowers, including four different species of orchid. Leaflets are available to help identify the trees and animals you might spot along the way.

WALK DETAILS

Start/finish: Bedgebury National Pinetum and Forest, Lady Oak Lane, Goudhurst, TN17 2SJ

Distance: 2 miles (3.2km)

Difficulty: 2/5

Public transport: Train to Tunbridge Wells then number 254 bus from Tunbridge Wells. The nearest bus stop is Flimwell Corner Farm.

DIRECTIONS

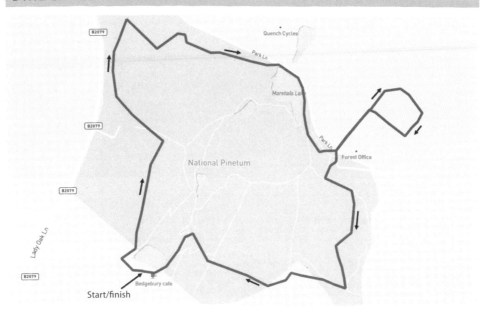

Start/finish

1. The Hidden Secrets trail is fully waymarked throughout. Follow waymarkers from the visitor centre and finish at the family-friendly cafe.

THINGS TO SEE AND DO NEARBY

Bedgebury is exciting to explore by bike, with several cycle trails heading off on longer adventures through the trees. Bikes, including trailers for younger children, are available to hire from a shop near the visitor centre.

The castles at **Bodiam**, **Sissinghurst** and **Scotney** are all nearby and make fantastic days out, all with excellent walks nearby.

36

The castle on the Weald at Sissinghurst

SISSINGHURST, KENT

Set in the High Weald of Kent, Sissinghurst Castle was the 1930s home of poet and writer Vita Sackville-West, and her diplomat and author husband Harold Nicolson. Together, they transformed the former manor house and its garden into a celebration of their combined creative vision.

Today, Sissinghurst's famous gardens are a delight to walk around, drawing in even the youngest children, who can watch bees busy in the flowers and explore the many paths through the different gardens and orchard. While the house and gardens are National Trust membership/paid entry, most of the 450-acre estate surrounding the castle is free to explore.

This walk takes you from the castle out alongside the intriguing moat and past the gardens to explore Roundshill Park Wood. Follow the main path along the edge of the woodland, or plunge deeper into the trees, looking for fungi, birds and invertebrates as you go. Whether you visit in autumn when the trees shine with colour, in winter when the fallen leaves crunch beneath your feet, or in spring and summer when the leafy canopy glows green, it's a lovely place in which to wander.

The little gazebo, at the start of the walk, is a memorial to Harold Nicolson that was commissioned by his sons. It was designed by the architect Francis Pym in 1969 with the exact same dimensions as the *Apollo 11* lunar module, which made the first human landing on the moon in the same year.

WALK DETAILS

Start/finish: Sissinghurst Castle, Biddenden Road, TN17 2AB

Distance: 1 mile (1.6km)

Difficulty: 1/5

Public transport: Regular service to Staplehurst from London Charing Cross. From here, take bus service 5 to Sissinghurst.

DIRECTIONS

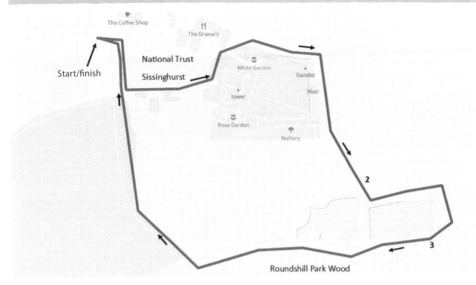

The Coffee Shop

The Granary

National Trust
Sissinghurst

Start/finish

White Garden

Gazebo

Tower

Moat

Rose Garden

Nuttery

2

3

Roundshill Park Wood

1. Leave the car park, following the main path towards the castle. Walk to the left of the castle and alongside the moat, following it round to the right, past the gazebo, through a gate and down the hill towards the lake.

2. At the bottom of the field, go through the gate and turn left to walk around the lower lake.

3. After crossing the second bridge, turn right and follow the path along the edge of the woodland at Roundshill Park Wood. After a short distance you will reach a marker with an 'F' on it. You can either turn right for the 1-mile (1.6km) walk, crossing Park Field to return to the castle and car park or, to extend the walk, continue through the woodland until you reach a 'G' marker. Turn right here and follow the footpath across fields to reach the main driveway, then turn right and follow this back to the castle.

THINGS TO SEE AND DO NEARBY

The romantic, part-ruined, 14th-century moated **Scotney Castle** is nearby. Surrounded by 780 acres of rolling parkland, this makes a fantastic day out, offering many walks of differing lengths.

Near to Scotney, **Bewl Water** is the largest stretch of open water in the South East. Set within an 800-acre site in the heart of the High Weald, it's an excellent location for walking, cycling and watersports, and also has a cafe and campsite.

SOUTH EAST ENGLAND

97

CENTRAL ENGLAND AND EAST ANGLIA

A waterfall walk from Carding Mill Valley

SHROPSHIRE HILLS, SHROPSHIRE

The Shropshire Hills Area of Outstanding Natural Beauty covers a vast, wild corner of south-west Shropshire, including a stretch along the Welsh borders. Within easy reach of many of the Midlands' towns and cities, it feels like a wild and adventurous escape. Although it's a popular family destination, most don't stray far from the main areas, and there are plenty of quieter, wilder parts within easy walking distance.

Carding Mill Valley is an ideal place to start your explorations of the Shropshire Hills and you'll also find a cafe and car park here. There's a stream for paddling and playing in, and inviting hilltops all around. Our choice of walk is a simple but exhilarating out-and-back excursion, starting in the heart of the valley and following the course of the river upstream to discover the magical Light Spout Waterfall. Filling the air with its incessant music, a cascade of water spills through a rocky cleft and into a clear pool below. Listen out for the clink of stonechats, the purr of ravens and the mew of circling buzzards as you go.

Further afield in the Shropshire Hills there's plenty more to explore. Take in the far-reaching views to the mountains of Snowdonia from the summit of Brown Clee Hill which, at 1,791 feet (546 metres), is also the highest point in Shropshire, or visit the Bronze Age Bodbury Ring and the expansive Long Mynd. It's also a great car-free destination since Church Stretton train station takes you right into the middle of it all.

WALK DETAILS

Start/finish: Carding Mill Valley National Trust Car Park, Church Stretton, SY6 6JG

Distance: 2 miles (3.2km)

Difficulty: 3/5

Public transport: Trains to Church Stretton, 1 mile (1.6km) from the start

DIRECTIONS

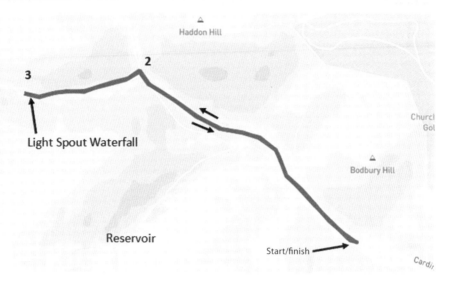

Haddon Hill

2

3

↓

Light Spout Waterfall

←
→

**Church
Gol**

Bodbury Hill

Reservoir

Start/finish ➤

Cardi

1 Walk up past both car parks, following the main track and red waymarkers along the left side of the stream.

2 A little further up the valley, the path forks. Take the left-hand fork away from the main valley and into the narrow V-shaped valley of Lightspout Hollow. In summer, you can forage for bilberries – tiny, wild blueberries – on the low bushes that cloak the hillsides.

3 Follow the steepening path up to reach the waterfall, which is particularly spectacular after heavy rainfall. With strong walkers, you can continue up the path alongside the waterfall and up to the ridge at Shooting Box. Otherwise, retrace your steps down the valley to the car park.

THINGS TO SEE AND DO NEARBY

There's a fantastic network of bridleways in this area, perfect for discovering on two wheels. The **Shropshire Hills Mountain Bike and Outdoor Pursuit Centre** offers bike hire, trail maps, a shop and a repairs centre.

A wildlife wander up Garway Hill

GARWAY, HEREFORDSHIRE

Herefordshire is among England's least-populous counties, nestled near to the Welsh borders in an area known as The Marches. The varied landscape of gently rolling countryside, woodland and farmland, cut through by the beautiful River Wye, lends itself to wilder walks.

Garway Hill lies south of Hereford, near to the market town of Ross-on-Wye. It is an area of open common land, great for flying kites and crisscrossed by inviting trails. The walking is straightforward and enjoyable at any time of year and an ascent is richly rewarded with views across five counties on a clear day, including the Black Mountains and the distinctive tree-topped May Hill in Gloucestershire, the destination for our next walk.

On top of Garway Hill stands the remains of a Second World War radio tracking station that once stood around 26 feet (8 metres) high. Just short of the summit lies the mysterious Black Pool, which, despite having no obvious source, is always full and provides water for the sheep and ponies that graze the common. It's also a breeding spot for great crested newts, a protected native species that, with their warty skin and wavy crests, resemble miniature dinosaurs.

Other fascinating wildlife includes a number of endangered birds, including skylarks and bullfinches; the mud snail, which is extinct in much of lowland Britain; and glow-worms, whose glowing displays are best seen in the evenings during late June and early July.

WALK DETAILS

Start/finish: Lower Castre parking area, Garway, nearest postcode HR2 8RU; grid ref SO443247

Distance: 1.2 miles (1.9km)

Difficulty: 2/5

Public transport: On school days, a bus runs from Hereford, where there's a train station, to Garway and back, giving you a good day's exploring in between

DIRECTIONS

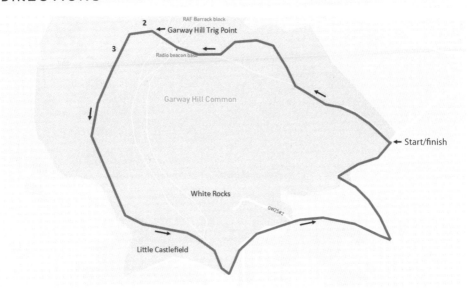

RAF Barrack block
2 ← Garway Hill Trig Point
3
Radio beacon base

Garway Hill Common

← Start/finish

White Rocks

GW25#2

Little Castlefield

1 From the parking area, follow the main path north-west up Garway Hill. As you approach the top, marked with a hexagonal building – a former Second World War radio tracker station – you will pass Black Pool.

2 Take some time to enjoy the views from the summit, out across five counties if you're lucky enough to visit on a clear day. West towards the Black Mountains you can see the distinctive wedge-shaped hills of Sugar Loaf (Walk 77) and Skirrid (Walk 78).

3 Continue straight over from the summit, picking your way through the maze of paths. Bear left before you reach the bottom of the hill and contour around the lower slopes until you reach the lane below White Rocks. Turn left here, either detouring up to explore White Rocks or following the lane back to the parking area.

THINGS TO SEE AND DO NEARBY

The nearby ruined castles at **Skenfrith** and **Grosmont** are both fascinating to explore and free to enter. The towering crags and rocky ravine at **Symonds Yat** offer a vast number of activities, from rock climbing and kayaking to woodland wanders and peregrine falcon spotting.

Run for the trees on May Hill

MAY HILL, GLOUCESTERSHIRE

The rolling landscape of north-west Gloucestershire is patchworked with grassy fields and woodland. Rising to just short of 984 feet (300 metres), with its distinctive clump of trees on its summit, May Hill is a visible landmark from many miles away in all directions. It therefore makes sense that the views, seen from within that magical miniature woodland at the summit, are stunning – particularly on a sparkling winter's morning when snow tops the distant Black Mountains, making them appear so clear they seem almost within touching distance. Looking 360 degrees from the trig point, you can also see the Malvern Hills, the Cotswolds, the Severn Vale and the Forest of Dean.

May Hill has drawn people to its viewpoint for millennia. As you ascend, you'll cross a circular trench, about 328 feet (100 metres) in diameter. This is thought to date back to the Iron Age, while the trees at the top were planted in 1887 to commemorate the golden jubilee of Queen Victoria. A local folk tradition sees Morris troupes from Gloucester and the Forest of Dean, along with residents from the surrounding counties of Gloucestershire and Herefordshire, visiting the hill to celebrate the sunrise each May Day.

May Hill Common – which is looked after by the National Trust – covers more than 70 acres of common land, and commoners still graze their ponies, pigs and sheep amid the birch, oak and crab apple trees.

WALK DETAILS

Start/finish: May Hill Common, nearest postcode GL18 1JS; grid ref SO690221

Distance: 3 miles (4.8km)

Difficulty: 3/5

Public transport: Trains to Gloucester then Stagecoach bus to Huntley, 1.5 miles (2.4km) from the start

DIRECTIONS

1 Leaving the parking area, head up the middle path to the top of May Hill Common. Go through the kissing gate at the end of the wall, which marks the county boundary, heading for the clump of pine trees.

2 From the pine trees, follow the main track to the southern end of the hill, going through a gate and continuing along the track straight over the crossroads.

3 Take the next left and follow the public footpath waymarkers to a small road. Turn left here, following a forestry track into the woodlands of the Huntley Estate.

4 Follow the public footpath signs through the woods; the footpath leaves the forestry track at times. You'll pass through a plantation of redwood trees. After this, continue straight ahead where two footpaths lead to the right. Carry straight on until a stile takes you back on to the common.

5 Carry on following the footpath across the common until it brings you out at the road just below the parking area.

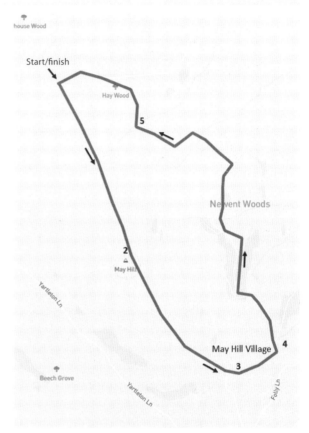

THINGS TO SEE AND DO NEARBY

The beautiful, part-ruined medieval castle at **Goodrich** (English Heritage membership/paid entry) is well worth a visit.

Symonds Yat, a rocky ravine where the River Wye carves its way through the limestone landscape, offers many exciting walks, adventure sports and the opportunity to watch peregrine falcons.

Between two counties on the Worcestershire Beacon

MALVERN HILLS, HEREFORDSHIRE/ WORCESTERSHIRE

The Malvern Hills are made from some of the most ancient rocks in England, formed an incredible 680 million years ago. The distinctive, undulating ridge of the hills runs for 9 miles (14.5km) end to end along the border between the counties of Worcestershire and Herefordshire, taking in 15 summits along the way.

The uplands are open grass and heath, while the lower slopes and steep valleys are wooded with ancient broadleaf. It's a good climb to the ridge from any of the car parks or the nearby train station in central Malvern, but the views of the surrounding countryside are well worth it and the walking is predominantly on well-maintained, easy-to-follow trails. The site is both an Area of Outstanding Natural Beauty and a Site of Specific Scientific Interest, so keep your eyes peeled for wildlife, including many species of wildflowers and birds, and perhaps even a little owl if you're lucky.

This walk climbs to the highest point on the hills – the Worcestershire Beacon at 1,394 feet (425 metres). However, by starting at Upper Wyche, where there's a saddle in the hills, you've gained much of the height before you even

WALK DETAILS

Start/finish: Beacon Road Upper or Lower Car Park, Upper Wyche, Malvern, WR14 4EH

Distance: 2.3 miles (3.7km)

Difficulty: 4/5

Public transport: Trains to Great Malvern or Colwall train stations. Buses from central Malvern to Upper Wyche.

begin walking. The Worcestershire Beacon can also be enjoyably walked from the train stations at Colwall or Great Malvern, although this will add a couple of miles and a quite a bit of extra ascent.

Once you get there, take the time to explore the summit, which has a long history as a signalling beacon. A notable example occurred in 1588, when it was once in a chain of warning fires that were lit when the Spanish Armada attempted to invade England. The toposcope at the beacon's summit identifies all the hills that can be seen on a clear day and was designed by Arthur Troyte Griffith – a friend of the composer Sir Edward Elgar, who grew up in the area and took inspiration for his music from the hills.

DIRECTIONS

1 Walk uphill from the parking area, following the main track for a short distance until you can bear left into a wooded area, then take the path through trees above the road and houses to your left.

2 Stay right at the next parking area, following the footpath that runs to the right of some large houses. Continue along the clear track as it curves around to the right, ascending to a major path junction in the coombe between North Hill and the Worcestershire Beacon.

3 Turn right at the path junction, following the main path up the ridge to the summit of the Worcestershire Beacon, which is marked by a large toposcope.

4 From the summit, continue in the same direction, following the main path south all the way back down to Beacon Road parking area.

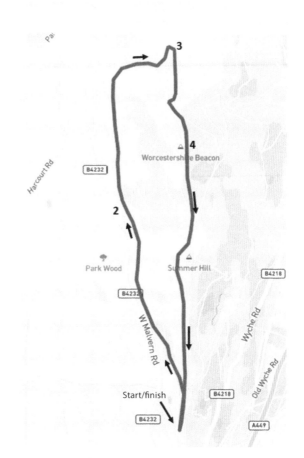

THINGS TO SEE AND DO NEARBY

Neighbouring **North Hill** makes an excellent extension to this walk, with an out-and-back adding only about an extra 1 mile (1.6km) in total.

The **British Camp** – also known as the **Herefordshire Beacon** – with its intriguing earthworks, the remnants of an Iron Age hill fort, is another great summit for kids.

Eastnor Castle, to the south, makes a great family day out; ticket purchase is required for entry.

A beacon and a bunker at Broadway Tower

BROADWAY, WORCESTERSHIRE

Broadway Tower stands proudly on a high point of the Cotswold escarpment. Set within a 50-acre estate, the tower is privately owned and payment is required to go inside. However, it's free to wander along the Cotswold Way that leads up to it, and the walk there and back from the pretty village of Broadway is delightful, with a long, downhill finish.

Imagined by the great 18th-century landscape designer Capability Brown and built by renowned architect James Wyatt for Lady Coventry, the Saxon-style tower overlooks an ancient trading route and was completed in 1798. It is said that Lady Coventry wished to be able to see the beacon from her other estate at Croome, 22 miles (35km) away.

Over the years, Broadway Tower has been used as a printing press, an artists' retreat and, in the late 1950s, a nuclear fallout monitoring station; the Royal Observer Corps nuclear bunker was built near to the tower, one of the last such Cold War bunkers constructed. Although it was officially stood down in 1991, it remains one of the few fully equipped facilities in England and is open to paying visitors over the summer months, although children under 10 are not permitted to enter. There is also a family- and dog-friendly cafe and parking on site if you'd prefer to walk around the tower rather than making the walk up from Broadway.

WALK DETAILS

Start/finish: Leamington Road Car Park, Broadway, WR12 7ET

Distance: 2.7 miles (4.3km)

Difficulty: 4/5

Public transport: Buses link Broadway with train stations at Cheltenham, Pershore and Moreton-in-Marsh

DIRECTIONS

1 From the centre of Broadway, walk east up the High Street until you can turn right on to the waymarked Cotswold Way National Trail. Follow this out past some houses and into fields.

2 Follow the clear path uphill through fields, staying on the Cotswold Way all the way to the tower. The return trip follows your outward route all the way back down to Broadway village.

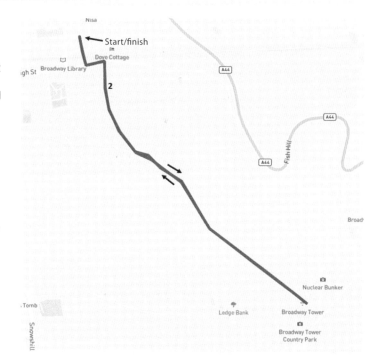

THINGS TO SEE AND DO NEARBY

Broadway village has plentiful cafes and independent food shops, perfect for putting together a picnic to take up the hill. Once you get to **Broadway Tower**, the newly opened visitor area has a shop, cafe, tours of the tower, estate and bunker and parking – paid entry.

A view from the fort at Haresfield Beacon

COTSWOLDS, GLOUCESTERSHIRE

Haresfield Estate covers nearly 300 acres of Cotswold countryside. Situated high on the Cotswold escarpment, inviting paths lead out over the grassy hillside with glorious views out across the Severn Estuary to the Black Mountains on the eastern edge of the Brecon Beacons, and to the Forest of Dean in Gloucestershire. If you're here with older children, the dramatic landscape makes for some challenging but adventurous walks, with winding woodland trails, steep climbs and descents, and springy open grassland.

A herd of black-and-white Belted Galloway cattle graze the grasslands around Haresfield, eating the tougher grasses and allowing wildflowers to thrive. Look out for plants such as thyme, vetch, marjoram and rare orchids, along with many birds and insects that make their homes here. Nearby Standish Wood is a lovely place to visit in spring and early summer, when the roots of the veteran beech trees – some more than 200 years old – are covered in bluebells and other flowers. There's also a fascinating number of archaeological features in the area, including long barrows and round barrows, a hill fort and a cross dyke, all of which are more than 3,000 years old.

This walk stays on top of the escarpment and provides fantastic views throughout. It visits the topograph-topped spur in front of Haresfield Camp, and the beacon on the opposite side of the steep-sided valley to the west.

WALK DETAILS

Start/finish: Shortwood National Trust Car Park, Cotswold Way, Stroud, GL6 6PP

Distance: 1.9 miles (3.1km)

Difficulty: 2/5

Public transport: Bus 93 Stroud to Gloucester stops on the A4173 at Scottsquar

DIRECTIONS

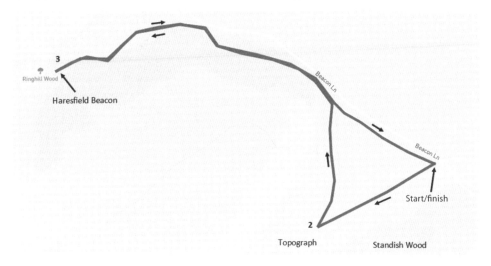

1   From the car park, go through the gate on to the grassland, following the Cotswold Way straight ahead towards the view and topograph.

2   From the topograph, turn your back on the view and follow the Cotswold Way to the left, along the edge of some woods. At the path junction, turn left, continuing along the Cotswold Way through woodland and around the edge of the escarpment until you reach the trig point at Haresfield Beacon.

3   From the beacon, return along the Cotswold Way until it curves to the right towards the topograph. Stay straight ahead here, leaving the Cotswold Way and crossing the grassland to return to your start point.

THINGS TO SEE AND DO NEARBY

Just south of Haresfield, across the River Severn, the secluded, wooded valley of **Woodchester Park** is an intriguing place to explore, with its excellent play trail, partly wild 18th- and 19th-century landscape park, romantic Victorian mansion and a string of five lakes at the heart of the valley.

Find your way at Piper's Hill and Hanbury Hall

HANBURY, WORCESTERSHIRE

This longer walk provides a good opportunity to get started in map or GPS navigation, with clear, well-marked footpaths to follow around an adventurous loop that takes in woodland, towpath and the parkland surrounding the National Trust's Grade I listed Hanbury Hall.

Also known as Hanbury Woods, Piper's Hill is one of the Wildlife Trusts' flagship nature reserves. Home to some of the oldest trees in the county, this is also an important area for wood pasture – a wildlife-rich network of woodland and grassland. By selectively removing new growth and introducing conservation grazing, the Wildlife Trusts are gradually restoring areas of wood pasture to the country. Look out for an abundance of wildlife in the woods, including more than 200 species of fungi, such as chanterelle, beefsteak and various bracket fungi.

This walk begins at Piper's Hill, winding through woodland before heading for Hanbury Church Hill, from the top of which are fine views out across the surrounding countryside. From here, there's a loop of the grassy trails around the National Trust's Hanbury Hall, a grand Georgian mansion surrounded by 400 acres of gardens and parkland. The final miles take you along a stretch of the Birmingham Canal, before heading back through fields to Piper's Wood.

WALK DETAILS

Start/finish: Piper's Hill free car park on the west side of the B4091, nearest postcode B60 4AS; grid ref SO957652

Distance: 5.5 miles (8.9km)

Difficulty: 3/5

Public transport: Train to Droitwich Spa, then bus to Gallows Green, 1.4 miles (2.3km) away

DIRECTIONS

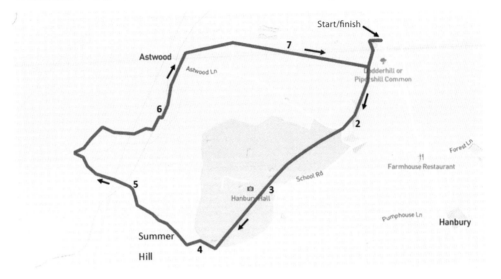

1   From the car park, follow the path downhill towards the pond, and south through the woods. At the end of the woodland, bear slightly right and follow the footpath through a field and up Hanbury Church Hill to the little church at the top.

2   Walk through the churchyard and out of the main entrance to reach a road. Follow this for a short distance until you can turn left on to a footpath descending to Hanbury Park. Go through the gate and stay left at the fork, passing two small ponds on your right, and carry on until you reach the front of Hanbury Hall.

3   Continue straight ahead, crossing the main driveway to the hall and following the footpath straight across the parkland to reach a small pond on your right and a lane. Go over the stile but not on to the lane; instead, take the footpath immediately right to reach a double stile. Turn left before the stile and follow the footpath along the edge of the field to a gap in the hedge and a footbridge.

4   Cross over the footbridge and follow the footpath to the right of Lacey Wood and to the left of Summerhill Wood, then down the hill to reach Summerhill Farm.

5   Follow the footpath round to the right of the farm to reach a bridge over the Birmingham Canal. You can either access the towpath here or cross over the footbridge and follow the footpath until it crosses a bridleway to Walmer Farm. Turn right, go under the railway and walk back to the canal, where you'll cross on a lock gate with a handrail – this is fun for children but will require careful supervision.

6   Follow the towpath north until you reach Astwood Lane Bridge. Go under the bridge, then turn right over a stile and follow a footpath east across fields with stiles and footbridges to reach a country lane. Turn right on to the lane and then left on to another footpath, following this through fields to a footbridge over a stream.

7   Cross this and continue until you reach your outbound path at Piper's Hill, following this back to the car park.

THINGS TO SEE AND DO NEARBY

Hanbury Hall is well worth a visit, and features a cafe, play trail and children's activities alongside a formal George London garden, with precise, geometric designs.

Nearby **Croome**, also National Trust, is another great place to visit, with many buggy-friendly paths and trails to explore.

The mystery of the Four Stones at Clent

CLENT, WORCESTERSHIRE

The Clent Hills offer a haven of green rolling countryside in the heart of the busy West Midlands. Networked with footpaths, trails and bridleways, they can be explored on foot or mountain bike. On a clear day, the short, steep climbs are handsomely rewarded with views from the tops across to the Malvern Hills, the Cotswolds, the Shropshire Hills and the Black Mountains of the Welsh borders.

The hills are dotted with many fascinating echoes of those who have lived here over the centuries, including an Iron Age hill fort on Wychbury Hill. There are also a number of 18th-century follies, which were commissioned by the Lyttelton family, builders of the neo-Palladian mansion of Hagley Hall located to the north-west of the hills, whose ancestors still live in the Hall today. While exploring the hills, it's worth looking out for some of these follies, such as the Rotunda; the delicate and sadly much-vandalised remains of a Palladian bridge; Jacob's Well; Thomson's Seat; the Temple of Theseus; and Hagley Castle, a mock castle situated in Hagley Park and visible from the hills.

This enjoyable walk starts with a climb up a woodland trail to reach a fine viewpoint and the site of another of the Lytteltons' commissions, the Four Stones, on Clent Hill. This atmospheric site feels ancient and peaceful, despite only having been constructed in 1763. A cold, clear winter evening is a perfect time to visit, when the setting sun casts long shadows across the hillside.

WALK DETAILS

Start/finish: Nimmings Wood Cafe, Clent, DY9 9JR

Distance: 1.9 miles (3.1km)

Difficulty: 2/5

Public transport: Buses to Hagley, a 1-mile (1.6km) walk from the start

DIRECTIONS

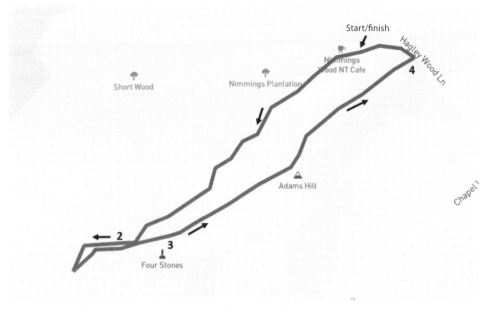

1. From the cafe, follow the zigzag path up the hill into woodland, bearing right and continuing along an easy-access path with plenty of places to stop and take in the views along the way.

2. Leaving the woods, turn left and walk up to the Four Stones.

3. From the Stones, walk to the left of the clump of trees and through a gate into Horse's Mane Woodland. Follow the path past 250-year-old pollarded beech trees, which were kept cut short so that new shoots would provide reachable food for livestock.

4. At the end of the woods, bear left to return to the cafe.

THINGS TO SEE AND DO NEARBY

The further reaches of the **Clent Hills** are wonderful to explore, with great views, well-maintained trails and lots of intriguing points of historical and cultural significance.

Nimmings Wood Cafe is an ideal finishing point for a brisk walk on the hills, serving a good range of food and drink. Cash only.

Discover an urban wilderness at Sutton Park

SUTTON PARK, BIRMINGHAM

Covering some 2,400 acres of wild land just a few miles north of Birmingham city centre, Sutton Park is one of Europe's largest urban parks, providing a precious breathing space for those who live in the surrounding towns and cities. A designated Site of Special Scientific Interest and a National Nature Reserve, this former hunting forest offers a wealth of wonderful walking through ancient oak and birch woods, over heather-clad heathland, wetlands, marshes and around its lakes and pools, all important habitats for a diverse variety of wildlife. You might also spot cattle and wild ponies grazing on the land – these are part of a carefully managed conservation grazing programme to keep invasive plant species at bay on the open heathland.

Several of the lakes, including Keeper's Pool and Wyndley Pool, both of which are passed on this walk, were built in the Middle Ages to stock fish. The pools were made by damming small streams, and both the dam and the quarry used for their construction are still visible today.

This lovely loop is smooth and accessible and makes an excellent gentle 3.1-mile (5km) jog with a running buggy, too. It starts and finishes at the visitor centre, where there's a range of facilities as well as maps of the park, including lots of other great walks.

WALK DETAILS

Start/finish: Park Road, Sutton Coldfield, B73 6BT. This walk can also be accessed from Boldmere Gate or Streetly Gate.

Distance: 3.1 miles (5km)

Difficulty: 2/5

Public transport: Regular buses and trains from central Birmingham to Sutton Coldfield. The train station is a short walk from the start.

DIRECTIONS

1 With the visitor centre on your left, take the left-hand fork, then keep on the right-hand path towards Wyndley Pool. Pass the pool on your left and continue straight ahead through Hollyhurst. Look out for holly blue butterflies here over the summer months.

2 At the fork, take the sharp right-hand path, then, at the next two junctions, take the left-hand path leading uphill.

3 At the next junction, which is Flying Field, turn right and follow the path across heathland, ascending gently towards the Jamboree Stone. From the Stone, bear left at the fork, following the path downhill and passing Keeper's Well and Keeper's Pool on your left to reach a metal gate. Go through the gate and follow the path back to the visitor centre.

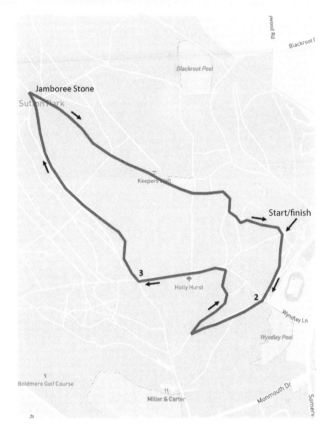

THINGS TO SEE AND DO NEARBY

There's a lot more to discover at Sutton Park, including learning to sail at **Powell's Pool** with **Sutton Sailing Club** and kayaking at **Blackroot Pool** with the **Royal Sutton Coldfield Canoe Club**. There are also two **orienteering courses**, available September to April, to avoid disturbing ground nesting birds.

A stepping stones walk at Dovedale

PEAK DISTRICT, DERBYSHIRE

Dovedale is one of those places that simply inspires children. Here, the tranquil River Dove winds its way through high limestone hills dotted with pockets of ravine woodland. The place names – Lover's Leap, Tissington Spires, Jacob's Ladder and Reynard's Cave – have a wonderful air of mystery, while the sparklingly clear water and inviting trails are just calling out to be explored.

Set in the White Peak area of the Peak District, just across the Derbyshire border into Staffordshire, Dovedale and neighbouring Ilam occupy two parallel river valleys whose rivers – the Manifold and the Dove – confluence just to the south. Much of the area is a National Trust nature reserve. It's a popular place, with good reason, so if you can visit away from the busiest times you'll make the most of the natural features. An early morning visit, returning to the car park just as everyone else is arriving, is a very special thing.

This walk starts at the southern end of Dovedale and climbs to the summit of Thorpe Cloud. The mini mountain is a reef knoll, a hill of calcareous matter that would originally have collected on an ancient sea floor. The views are well worth the climb, which, while steep, is straightforward and not overly long. If you prefer, you can make the walk a very pleasant and much flatter out-and-back along the river. Once you have descended the far side of Thorpe Cloud you'll reach the famous stepping stones, where it's all too easy to spend the rest of the day playing.

WALK DETAILS

Start/finish: Dovedale National Trust Car Park, Ilam, Ashbourne, DE6 2AY

Distance: 1.2 miles (1.9km)

Difficulty: 4/5 via Thorpe Cloud or 2/5 out-and-back along the river

Public transport: Regular buses between Ashbourne and Buxton stop nearby

CENTRAL ENGLAND AND EAST ANGLIA

DIRECTIONS

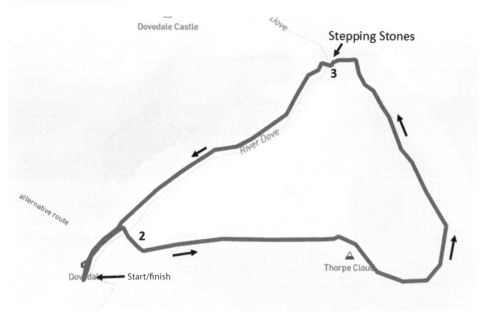

1 From the car park, head uphill along the signed path towards Dovedale. After a short distance, turn right over a footbridge to reach the bottom of the hill at Thorpe Cloud. If you would prefer not to make the climb, continue along the main path that follows the River Dove all the way to the stepping stones.

2 Otherwise, follow the steep path up Thorpe Cloud to the summit and, once you've taken a moment to admire the views, continue on the obvious path down the other side, bearing left towards the bottom to reach the river and stepping stones.

3 Cross the stepping stones and turn left once you reach the opposite bank. Follow this path all the way back to the car park.

THINGS TO SEE AND DO NEARBY

The National Trust-owned **Ilam Park** is a great extension to the walk and you can explore much of the estate for free.

Further along the River Manifold, near to the village of Wetton, is the impressive **Thor's Cave** – a gaping hole that rises above the wooded hillside. For those with sure feet and a good head for heights, it's a fun scramble up to the cave and exciting to explore.

Take in the views from the top of Mam Tor

PEAK DISTRICT, DERBYSHIRE

The airy summit of Mam Tor – meaning 'Mother Hill' – rises to 1,696 feet (517 metres) above the Vale of Edale in the Dark Peak region, one of a series of tors set along a soaring ridge that extends north-east to Lose Hill. The whole ridge makes an outstanding walk for older children, and we've included the directions for this opposite, but the simple ascent of the stone-clad path from Mam Nick Car Park to the top and back is a perfect way to get started. Either way, you'll be greeted by some of the finest views in the Peak District, stretching out across Edale, the Hope Valley and to the edge of the Kinder Scout plateau, along with a real feeling of being high up in a wild, mountain world.

Mam Tor has the nickname the 'Shivering Mountain' thanks to its history of landslips that sent loose shale and gritstone sliding down its sides. A long history of human habitation can still be seen etched into the hill, from finds of Neolithic flints, through two Bronze Age round barrows towards the summit, to the Iron Age earthworks that enclose an area of about 6 hectares and would once have been a large hill fort. Should you find yourself there in winter, it's a popular sledging spot, too.

WALK DETAILS

Start/finish: Mam Nick Car Park, Sheffield Road, Castleton, S33 8WA

Distance: 3 miles (4.8km)

Difficulty: 4/5

Public transport: Mam Tor bus stop not in use at time of writing. Bus to Castleton then a 1-mile (1.6km) walk. Nearest train stations at Hope and Edale.

DIRECTIONS

1 From the top of the car park, go up the steps and follow the path alongside the road to a small gate and National Trust sign. Go through the gate and bear left, following first some steps and then a flagstone path to reach the trig point-topped summit.

2 Continue along the flagstone path northwards along the ridge until you reach a small monument. Turn right here, walking downhill towards little Mam Tor. Just before the trees, bear right at the fork, skirting the woods to reach a road.

3 Follow the road through a gate and continue along the broken surface, caused by a landslide. Go through a gate and parking area then turn left down a track to Blue John Cavern (paid entry/ not National Trust).

4 Walk past the entrance, through a small gate and up a grassy path. Bear right at the top of the hill and go through a gate, crossing a field and road and bearing left at the fork. Follow the path uphill to another cave, Windy Knoll. Caution: rockfall, do not enter the cave.

5 From Windy Knoll, walk across the field to a small gate by the road. Cross the road and walk along the verge back to the car park.

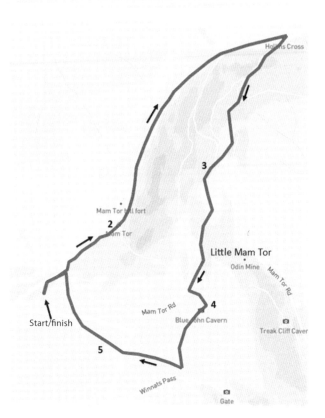

THINGS TO SEE AND DO NEARBY

Make a trip to the National Trust-owned **Penny Pot Cafe** in nearby Edale, from where there are some incredible walks out along the Pennine Way.

Visit the dramatic ruins of **Peveril Castle** (English Heritage membership/paid entry) near to the village of Castleton. Built by Henry II in 1176, the castle is one of England's earliest Norman fortresses.

Boggarts and Burbage Brook at Longshaw

PEAK DISTRICT, DERBYSHIRE

Boggarts are popular in folklore, particularly further north in England, and in children's literature – from Susan Cooper's 'The Boggart' to the shape-shifting terrors of the Harry Potter books. Definitions vary, but they're often mischievous, mysterious and usually appear either indoors – as house fairies that sour milk and make things disappear – or outdoors, hiding behind trees, in marshes or under bridges.

The Longshaw Estate covers 1,600 acres of wild moorland, rugged gritstone edges and peaceful woodland in the heart of the Peak District National Park. Networked with paths and trails, many of which are accessible, it's a wonderful place in which to discover spectacular views, paddle in the brook that runs through the estate, spot wildlife and, if you're lucky, even find some boggart houses.

There's some fascinating human history to discover at Longshaw, too, from the Bronze Age ring cairns and hut circles on the moors to the remnants of millstones that can be seen dotted across the estate. These date back to the 15th century, when millstones were made at Yarncliffe Quarry.

This walk follows the pink waymarked Burbage Brook trail around the estate, taking in woodland and following a stretch of the brook.

WALK DETAILS

Start/finish: Longshaw visitor centre and cafe, Longshaw, Sheffield, S11 7TZ

Distance: 1.7 miles (2.8km)

Difficulty: 3/5

Public transport: Grindleford train station is 1 mile (1.6km) away, or there are regular buses from Sheffield – alight at Fox House Inn near the estate entrance

DIRECTIONS

1 Leave the cafe, cross the drive and turn left to follow the path alongside the fence. Go through the gate and turn right, heading downhill until you reach Longshaw pond.

2 Continue following the path around the pond and down through Granby Wood with its towering Scots pine trees, which were planted in 1990. Pass Granby Barn and continue to a gate.

3 Go through the gate and cross the road, then cross the bridge over Burbage Brook. Turn right after the bridge and follow the riverside path until you can re-cross on a second footbridge.

4 Follow the footpath straight ahead, turn right at the next junction and walk uphill through woodland until you reach a white gate and a road. Cross the road (caution) and turn right, following the drive back to the cafe.

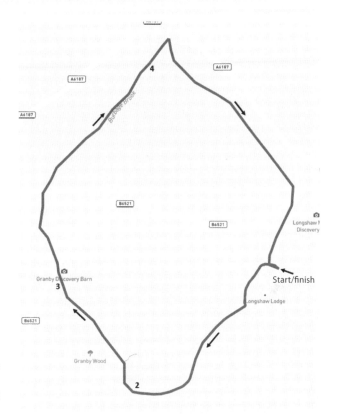

THINGS TO SEE AND DO NEARBY

There's a range of **waymarked, family-friendly walks** around the estate, many of which are accessible for buggies and wheelchairs. Pick up a leaflet at the visitor centre.

Follow an old railway along the Monsal Trail

BAKEWELL, DERBYSHIRE

The Monsal Trail is a 9-mile (14.5km) multi-user path that runs between Bakewell and Chee Dale, near Buxton, in the Peak District. Passing through spectacular Derbyshire scenery, including the much-photographed Headstone Viaduct at Monsal Head, the trail makes a great family day out, whether you're walking or cycling.

A former railway, complete with several tunnels, the line was transformed into a path by Sustrans in 2011. Near to where the trail meets the pretty market town of Bakewell is the former train station of Hassop, now a cafe, bike hire centre, bookshop and playground. This is an ideal place to start and finish a walk in the area, since there's plenty of parking and you can jump straight on to the Monsal Trail.

This walk takes in a brilliantly varied loop that showcases this part of the Peak. From Hassop, it follows the Monsal Trail into Bakewell, tracing the meanders of the River Wye through fields before heading up and over a stretch of wild and open moorland on a well-maintained bridleway. During the winter months there's often snow here, but it's rarely impassable, while over the summer there are wild raspberries to forage and an abundance of butterflies to spot, seeking out the wildflowers that flourish in the limestone landscape.

WALK DETAILS

Start/finish: Hassop Station cafe, Hassop Road, Bakewell, DE45 1NW

Distance: 3.3 miles (5.3km)

Difficulty: 3/5

Public transport: Bus 218 connects train stations at Sheffield and Matlock with Bakewell

CENTRAL ENGLAND AND EAST ANGLIA

DIRECTIONS

1 Turn left out of Hassop train station on to the Monsal Trail in the direction of Bakewell. Continue for about 1 mile (1.6km) until you reach the old train station at Bakewell. Turn right here, leaving the Monsal Trail and joining Station Road.

2 Follow Station Road downhill towards Bakewell until you reach a road junction with the road bridge over the River Wye to your left. Cross the road just before the bridge to reach a gate into fields. Follow the footpath through the fields with the river on your left until you reach a road – Holme Lane.

3 Turn left on to Holme Lane and follow it as it bends to the right, away from the river at a packhorse bridge. Follow the road uphill as it becomes a track, passing some disused mines on your right. Continue on this track up and over the open hillside, where there are wonderful views out across the surrounding White Peak countryside. Eventually, the track will bring you back down to meet the Monsal Trail.

4 Turn right on to the Monsal Trail and follow this back to Hassop Station cafe.

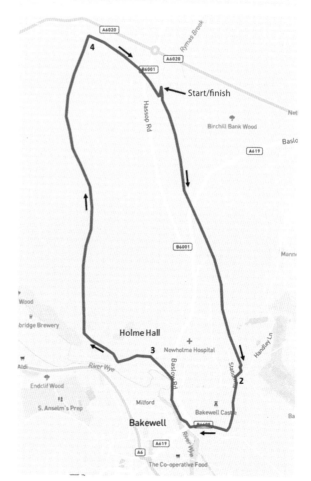

THINGS TO SEE AND DO NEARBY

Bakewell is a pleasant town to explore with children, whether you're watching shining trout swimming in the river or making use of the expansive play area to the south.

Nearby **Chatsworth** is also great for walking, with a thousand acres of deer park to discover and the River Derwent running through its centre. **Chatsworth House** is paid entry but the estate is free to walkers.

Cycling is another fun way to explore the **Monsal Trail**, wheeling through the echoing tunnels all the way to **Chee Dale**. There's a cafe at **Miller's Dale** and bike hire at both Hassop and Chee Dale.

Into the fens at Anglesey Abbey

ANGLESEY ABBEY, CAMBRIDGESHIRE

Anglesey Abbey has had a long and varied past. Built as a hospital in the 12th century, it was turned into an Augustinian Priory in the 13th century, dissolved by Henry VIII in the 16th century and then became a family home from the 17th century onwards. Standing within 114 acres of gardens and grounds on the outskirts of Lode in the Cambridgeshire fens, it's a wonderfully peaceful place to explore. The footpaths run in straight lines along the lodes – a series of man-made waterways thought to be Roman in origin – turning a right angle at each corner.

Nearby Wicken Fen is one of Europe's most important wetlands. Covering nearly 2,000 acres of wildflower meadows, grasslands, sedge and reed beds and networked by a series of boardwalks, it's an exciting place to explore. There's also plenty of wildlife to spot; the reserve is home to more than 9,000 different species, including a vast array of plants; birds, such as rare hen harriers, barn owls and bitterns; mammals, including water voles, badgers and bats; and insects, such as dragonflies. You might also see diminutive, semi-feral Konik ponies, which are part of a conservation project to create a diverse range of new habitats.

This walk explores the peaceful fenland and pretty Cambridgeshire villages near to Anglesey Abbey, visiting

WALK DETAILS

Start/finish: Anglesey Abbey National Trust Car Park, Quy Road, Lode, CB25 9EJ; grid ref TL533621

Distance: 4.6 miles (7.4km)

Difficulty: 3/5

Public transport: Bus services connect Cambridge train station with Anglesey Abbey

CENTRAL ENGLAND AND EAST ANGLIA

Stow-cum-Quy Fen – a designated Site of Special Scientific Interest for its diverse flora, including rare aquatic plants that flourish in a series of pools – and Lode Mill, an 18th-century watermill that was restored to working order in 1982 and still grinds grain into flour for local use and purchase today.

DIRECTIONS

1 Leave the car park through the furthest left corner from the road, join a footpath and follow it along the edge of a field and through a gate. Bear left along a path behind the tennis courts and allotments of Anglesey Abbey, then left again on to a narrow path to Lode Mill.

2 Cross the footbridge next to the mill, then turn left and follow the path alongside Quy Water, towards Stow-cum-Quy, until you reach a road. Don't go on to the road; instead, turn sharp right here, following signs to Quy Fen diagonally across a field and through a gate.

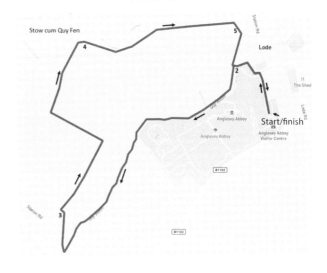

3 Turn right on to a bridleway and follow this as it becomes a gravel track. Bear right at the fork and continue along the path until you reach Quy Fen, then go through the gate and take the path across a field towards Lode, keeping to the right. Continue along the grass path until you reach a gate and footbridge at the end of Quy Fen.

4 Cross the bridge and go straight ahead, following the footpath across fields to join Head Fen Drove, a wide track. Follow this straight ahead until you reach a crossroads. Turn right here, stepping over a metal bar next to a gate.

5 Follow the path right and around the field back to Lode Mill. From here, retrace your steps along the path, past the allotments and alongside the field to reach the Anglesey Abbey Car Park and visitor centre.

THINGS TO SEE AND DO NEARBY

Wicken Fen has four open-fronted shelters – only accessible by walking or cycling – which are available to hire for camping. Each shelter sleeps six adults or eight children, with no tent required, and bookings are for the whole site. This makes for a real adventure for small groups and families.

Stroll along the sands at Anderby Creek

LINCOLNSHIRE COAST, LINCOLNSHIRE

The Lincolnshire Coastal Country Park was created to provide a diverse range of sustainable wildlife habitats, while at the same time supporting the local economy and supplying educational and recreational opportunities for people. Stretching across 5 miles (8km) of sandy beach backed by dunes and wetlands, this is an excellent spot for walking, wildlife spotting and playing on the beach.

This walk begins at Anderby Creek, on the coast, 5 miles (8km) north of the larger Chapel St Leonards. There's a basic shop and cafe at the start, along with the Cloud Bar, a purpose-built sky-gazing station complete with a guide to spotting clouds. From here, it follows the England Coast Path along an inland path through trees, dunes and fields to reach the nature reserve at Huttoft. An area of sea bank clay pits, which provided clay for sea bank repairs after the storm surge of 1953, this is now a wetland area with reed beds and a large area of open water. Use the hide to look for birds such as moorhens, water rails, reed and sedge warblers and many different species of duck. If you're lucky you might see or hear short-eared owls and bitterns during the winter months, and marsh harriers in spring.

Sea buckthorn, a spiny deciduous shrub with silvery leaves, grows across the sand dunes along this part of the coast. The orange berries are popular with many birds and can be used in cooking. Also known as the Siberian pineapple, it's said to be a good source of vitamin C.

WALK DETAILS

Start/finish: Car park, Sea Road, Anderby Creek, PE24 5XW

Distance: 3.5 miles (5.6km)

Difficulty: 2/5

Public transport: Buses from Skegness, where there's a train station, to Anderby Creek

DIRECTIONS

1 From the beach cafe, with the sea to your right, follow the track running past the car park and then a row of bungalows. Continue straight on through a small area of sycamore trees, then bear right to reach a track along the base of the dunes – an area known as Moggs Eye.

2 Continue along this track through Marsh Yard Car Park and picnic site, then bear left to follow the England Coast Path behind the dunes and along the edge of a field. At the end of the field, cross the bridge and continue straight on until you reach Huttoft Marsh nature reserve and the road.

3 Turn right on to Huttoft Car Terrace and continue to the beach. Turn right and walk along the beach for approximately 1.75 miles (2.8km) back to Anderby Creek, with its row of dune-top houses. Turn right past the Cloud Bar to return to your start point.

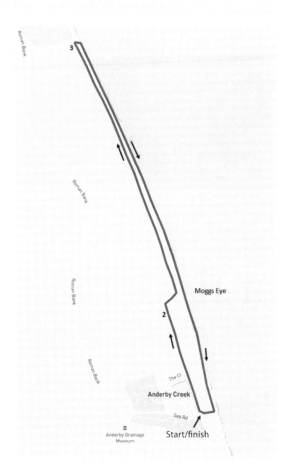

THINGS TO SEE AND DO NEARBY

To the south of Anderby Creek, the beach continues enjoyably towards **Chapel St Leonards**. This makes an excellent alternative walk, or an extension to the one described. There are further nature reserves at **Wolla Bank** and **Chapel Pit** along the way.

Seals and sandcastles at Holkham

HOLKHAM, NORFOLK

North Norfolk is an area of vast, sweeping sandy beaches edged with sand dunes, scented pinewoods, wildlife-rich marshlands and pretty villages. Holkham is one of the most spectacular, with a seemingly endless stretch of golden sand, magical saltwater lagoons and inviting boardwalk that leads through Corsican pines towards the sea. Like much of the landscape here, these trees are an echo of the centuries of battle between humans and the sea and were planted in the late 19th century to protect crops from the windblown sand.

This section of coastline is part of one of the largest National Nature Reserves in the country, and is home to rare and fascinating plant and animal life. If you're visiting in winter, look for flocks of migrant birds and thousands of pink-footed geese, white-fronted geese, brent geese and widgeon in the fields either side of Lady Anne's Drive. Over the summer months, you can find wild orchids, dark green fritillary butterflies, little and common terns at Wells Harbour, and a sea of purple lavender across the saltings.

This walk heads out along the beach and back along the Norfolk Coast Path through the pinewoods. Younger children may prefer a shorter loop of the beach – or, when the tide is out, it's exciting to simply walk as far as the sea.

WALK DETAILS

Start/finish: Lady Anne's Drive parking area, Holkham, nearest postcode NR23 1AB

Distance: 4 miles (6.4km)

Difficulty: 2/5

Public transport: Coastliner bus 36 links Fakenham with King's Lynn via Holkham and all minor stops. Hourly service.

DIRECTIONS

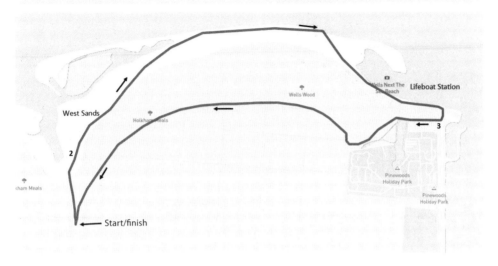

1 From the parking area near the visitor centre and cafe, follow a section of boardwalk through the pinewoods at Holkham Gap to reach first the lagoon and then the beach.

2 Turn right and follow the sands all the way to the end of Wells beach, passing a number of colourful beach huts just before you reach the end.

3 Pick up the Norfolk Coast Path at Wells and follow this all the way back to Holkham. There are lots of winding trails through the trees to explore further – or you could walk back the way you came along the beach.

THINGS TO SEE AND DO NEARBY

There's a wealth of cafes here, perfect for a warming hot chocolate after a winter adventure on the beach or an ice cream after some summer sandcastling. Choose from **The Lookout**, near to the parking area on Lady Anne's Drive, the **Courtyard Cafe** on Holkham Road, or the **Wells Beach Cafe** – a good halfway stop if you take on the full walk.

A glimpse of the past in Thetford Forest

THETFORD FOREST, NORFOLK/SUFFOLK BORDER

Planted just after the Second World War, in an effort to replace depleted timber supplies, Thetford Forest covers more than 46,000 acres of the Brecklands, which stretch across the borderlands of Norfolk and Suffolk. Divided into a number of different areas, each with its own history and points of interest, there's lots to explore around the forest and many miles of trails for walking, cycling and horse riding.

From around the 14th century, parts of the forest were used for rabbit farming, with vast warrens of hungry bunnies eating away the vegetation and creating sand dunes in places. Today, the landscape is very different, but the old tower at Thetford Warren Lodge – built by the Prior of Thetford in 1400 – still stands and is a fascinating insight into the farming practices of the past.

At Lynford, in another part of Thetford Forest, is one of the best-preserved late Middle Palaeolithic sites in Britain and the most important Neanderthal site in the country. A 2002 dig revealed evidence of human activity along with black flint hand axes and the fossilised remains of mammoths dating back 65,000 years.

This walk starts at High Lodge Visitor Centre and follows the waymarked Fir Trail throughout, winding through the more peaceful reaches of the forest, where beech trees blaze with colour over the autumn months.

WALK DETAILS

Start/finish: High Lodge Visitor Centre, Brandon, IP27 0AF

Distance: 3 miles (4.8km)

Difficulty: 2/5

Public transport: Train to Thetford then regular bus service to High Lodge

DIRECTIONS

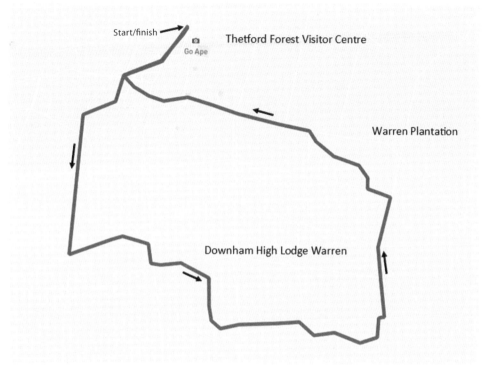

Start/finish

Go Ape

Thetford Forest Visitor Centre

Warren Plantation

Downham High Lodge Warren

1   From High Lodge Visitor Centre follow yellow waymarkers for the Fir Trail. This can be linked up with the Beech Trail at half-way for a longer walk, passing Thetford Warren Lodge.

THINGS TO SEE AND DO NEARBY

The recently opened **Heritage Trail** at High Lodge in Thetford Forest offers a multi-use, year-round circular route of 2.6 miles (4.2km) with two short cut options. A perfect way to explore with buggies and wheelchairs, it's a fascinating and engaging journey through the hidden history of the area and features interactive touchscreens and audio panels. You can also learn about wildlife conservation and timber production in the forest in two shelters along the way. **Thetford** is also fantastic for cycling – details and bike hire are available at the visitor centre.

History and heathland at Dunwich

DUNWICH, SUFFOLK

It is said that, with the right wind and tide, the church bells of the old town of Dunwich on the Suffolk coast can be heard ringing from far below the waves. Back in the 11th century, Dunwich was a bustling city with a population of around 4,000. With eight churches and a major trading port – where exports of wool and grain were exchanged for fish and timber – it was, at the time, busier than London. However, after a series of storms in the 13th and 14th centuries, people gradually moved away and the sea eventually claimed the old town. Recent ultrasound investigations of the seabed have found the ruins of churches, a toll house, pottery and several shipwrecks just off the coast. Settlement here has also been found to date back to the Iron Age, stretching through time to the nuclear power plant that now stands overlooking the North Sea at Sizewell, just to the south.

Today, Dunwich is a sleepy village with only around 50 permanent residents. Easy, level trails explore the peaceful pebble beach, heath and coastal lowlands, a haven for wildlife and a good place to spot many different birds. Wander around the nature reserve at Minsmere and you might see avocets, bearded tits and marsh harriers, or hear the lilting song of a nightingale or the booming call of a rare bittern.

WALK DETAILS

Start/finish: National Trust shop and tea room, Dunwich Heath, nearest postcode IP17 3DJ; grid ref TM476685

Distance: 3.3 miles (5.3km)

Difficulty: 3/5

Public transport: Not easily accessible by public transport. The nearest train station is Darsham, 6 miles (10km) away.

DIRECTIONS

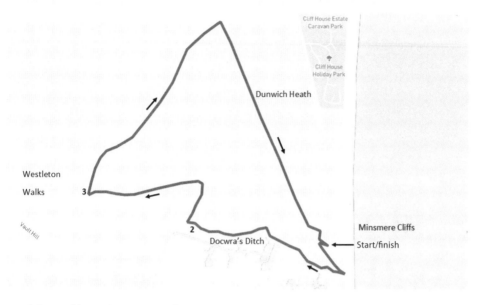

1. Turn left out of the parking area and follow the main coastal path down to the beach. From here, the Suffolk Coast Path runs southwards along the beach, edging Minsmere RSPB nature reserve. Turn right on to the beach and then take the first right, following Docwra's Ditch between Dunwich Heath and the nature reserve, keeping the ditch to your left.

2. Follow Docwra's Ditch as it heads around a 90-degree right-hand bend. Then, at the next path junction, turn left, leaving the ditch and taking the Sandlings Walk. Follow this through trees until a junction with a bridleway along an obvious track.

3. Turn right, leaving the Sandlings Walk and heading north, following the bridleway through trees and then out on to open heathland. Where the track forks, just after it crosses a ditch, bear right, staying on the bridleway. Then, where the Sandlings Walk joins the bridleway, turn right and follow this straight across the heath and back to the tea room.

THINGS TO SEE AND DO NEARBY

The **museum in Dunwich village** is filled with fascinating things, including a to-scale model of the 12th-century city, showing just how much of Dunwich lies under the sea.

Minsmere RSPB nature reserve is also a fantastic place to visit, and is home to a vast number of birds and also otters. You can join guided walks and safaris with local experts to find out more.

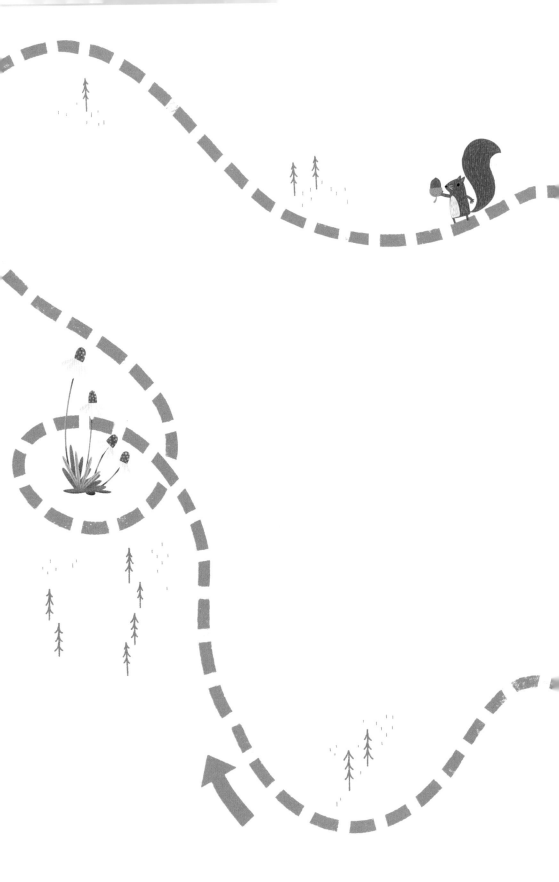

NORTH
ENGLAND

55

A red squirrel walk at Formby

FORMBY, MERSEYSIDE

Set on a sandy stretch of coastline between Southport in the north and Liverpool in the south, Formby is a little haven of peace and wildness with a fascinating history. It's a great winter destination, with its backdrop of evergreen pinewoods, and this is when the beach is at its quietest. On these days, gazing out across the sand to where the offshore wind turbines turn serenely out at sea, it's possible to imagine a time when humans will work with, rather than against, the natural world.

Until the 1990s, asparagus was grown at Formby, and most of the flat fields that are now grassed over still bear the furrows of many years of cultivation. The pinewoods that edge the coast were planted in the 1800s to offer protection for the crops – the dunes that would previously have been here are still visible between the trees. Today, the pinewoods are home to red squirrels, native to Britain but much reduced in numbers, particularly since the introduction of the grey squirrel from North America.

There are many options for shorter walks around Formby, but this one takes in a bit of everything so it's a good choice for kids who enjoy walking, with plenty to keep those who need some encouragement going, too. You'll pass the red squirrel woods, natterjack toad breeding grounds, former asparagus fields, sweeping coastal pinewoods, and the beach where you can spot prehistoric footprints and wander among the sand dunes.

WALK DETAILS

Start/finish: Formby National Trust Car Park, Victoria Road, Formby, L37 1LJ

Distance: 3 miles (4.8km)

Difficulty: 3/5

Public transport: Freshfield train station, on the Merseyrail Northern Line, is a 1-mile (1.6km) walk from the start

DIRECTIONS

1 From the car park, cross the road and take the Cornerstone path down the ramp into the woodland. Continue to follow the purple and white waymarkers through the woods until you reach a T-junction.

2 Turn right and follow the path waymarked 'Sefton Coastal Path' past the caravan park on your left. Carry on following the coastal path signs out of the woodland and into the dunes. As the path bends to the left, take the path straight ahead, leaving the Sefton Coastal Path and heading on to the beach.

3 Turn left and walk along the beach, keeping the dunes on your left. After approximately 0.75 miles (1.2km), turn left, following the Blundell Path marker back into the dunes. Take the next left into a vegetated area, following this around a right-hand bend and up a slope. When the path descends, bear right on to a clear path heading into a woodland of gnarled black poplar trees.

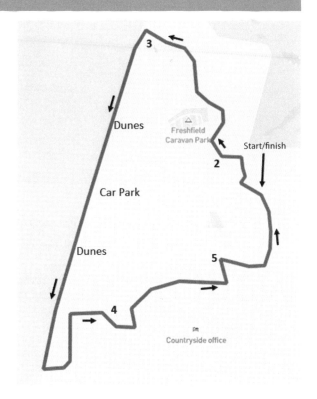

4 Bear right at the next fork, then turn right when you reach a T-junction. As this path curves to the right, take the sandy path on your left between two fenced fields. At the end of the fields, turn left and continue to a T-junction.

5 Turn right and walk through a small area of woodland and across a grassy field. At the end of the field, bear left up a stone path into the pinewoods. Follow this path until you reach a crossroads with a bench on your right. Go straight over here and around a left-hand bend, taking the next path right to return to the start.

THINGS TO SEE AND DO NEARBY

There's a **woodland play trail** near to the start of this walk.

Visit the site of prehistoric footprints at **Formby Point**. Created between 5,100 and 3,400 years ago, from the late Neolithic to the middle Bronze Age, these are an important source of information about early human settlement here. There are currently more than 220 identified trails of human footprints, along with animal prints from wild cattle, deer, wolves and wading birds.

56

The forgotten gardens at Rivington

BOLTON, LANCASHIRE

Set within easy reach of the M61 near to Bolton, Rivington Pike rises invitingly from the flanks of Winter Hill on the western edge of Lancashire's West Pennine moors. It was once owned by Lord Leverhulme, co-founder of the Lever Brothers soap empire, which became part of the global consumer goods company, Unilever. To the west of the Pike is the ruined maze of the Rivington Terraced Gardens, created by Leverhulme in the early 20th century with Japanese lakes, Romanesque bridges, stone archways, pagodas and even a ballroom. Abandoned in 1925, it has been taken over by nature and is a fascinating place to encounter part-ruined structures within the leafy woodland as you walk. Autumn is a particularly glorious time to visit, when the trees are ablaze with golden leaves and shafts of low sunlight stream through the masonry.

This walk follows easy trails through the gardens with plenty of opportunities to explore the various relics as you go. Emerging from the trees on to open hillside there's a final push to reach the summit of Rivington Pike, topped with Pike Tower, an 18th-century former hunting lodge. The views from the top, down to Rivington Reservoir and far beyond, are spectacular.

You may encounter vehicles on some of the road sections so be aware. While there's plenty of space, the final section can get busy during school holidays – and it's a local tradition to walk to the summit on Good Friday.

WALK DETAILS

Start/finish: Pigeon Tower Car Park, Belmont Road, Bolton, BL6 7SD

Distance: 1.9 miles (3.1km)

Difficulty: 3/5

Public transport: Regular buses from Bolton to Horwich, just south of Rivington

DIRECTIONS

1 Leave the car park and take the right-hand of the two tracks that lead up towards the woods, passing through a gate. Follow this uphill until you can turn left over an arched bridge.

2 Cross the bridge, then go up the steps and carry on uphill until you reach the main path, emerging from the woodland near to Pigeon Tower.

3 Turn right and follow the main track, bearing left to follow the obvious stepped path up to the summit of Rivington Pike.

4 The return walk can either retrace your outward steps or, on reaching the main path at point 3, turn right and follow this all the way back down to the car park.

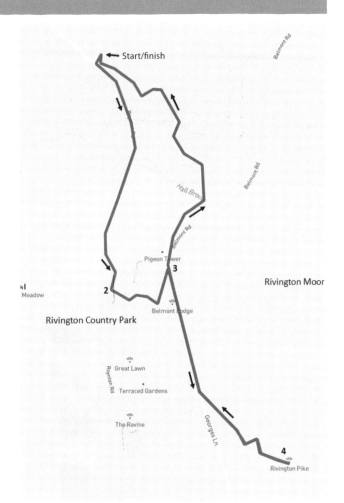

← Start/finish

Belmont Rd

Belmont Rd

Hall Brook

Belmont Rd

Pigeon Tower

3

2

Belmont Lodge

Rivington Moor

Rivington Country Park

Meadow

Great Lawn

Roynton Rd

Terraced Gardens

The Ravine

Georges Ln

4
Rivington Pike

THINGS TO SEE AND DO NEARBY

Great House Barn cafe on Rivington Lane is a beautiful cruck barn, built in 1706. A perfect spot for a post-walk hot chocolate or family lunch, you can also start your walk from here. This adds about 1 mile (1.6km) to the distance, all along bridleways.

57

Meander around Malham Tarn

YORKSHIRE DALES, NORTH YORKSHIRE

The Malham Tarn Estate, deep in the Yorkshire Dales, covers a dramatic, open limestone landscape of high fells, dry valleys, grassland and rocky outcrops. Nestled high in the fells above the village of Malham, the peaceful waters of Malham Tarn – a natural hollow in the underlying clay – and its surrounding area are a National Nature Reserve, internationally important for its wildlife.

The Pennine Way winds around the tarn's eastern shore making for easy walking or cycling in spectacular surroundings. This great out-and-back route takes you from the southern tip of the tarn around to the Field Centre at Malham Tarn House. For a longer walk or family-friendly cycle ride of about 4.5 miles (7.2km), you can continue on from the Field Centre and make a full circumnavigation of the tarn – a wonderful day out.

To the north-west of the tarn there's a long section of boardwalk crossing an area of wetland, which is really exciting for kids and a great place to spot some of the local birdlife. You might sight great crested grebes, tufted ducks, pochard, wigeon, teal, goosander and sometimes hen harriers. There are also a number of species of bat here; regular expert-led bat walks start at the Field Centre (pre-booking required).

WALK DETAILS

Start/finish: Watersinks Car Park, Malham Tarn, BD23 4DJ

Distance: 2.5 miles (4km) (1.25 miles/2km each way)

Difficulty: 2/5

Public transport: Buses to Malham village. Shuttle buses from Settle to Malham Tarn, summer weekends only.

DIRECTIONS

1 From the car park, follow the grassy path of the Pennine Way north. Go through a gate on to a track and follow this with the tarn to your left.

2 Continue following the main track through woodland and around the back of the Field Centre at Tarn House. From here, retrace your steps to the start.

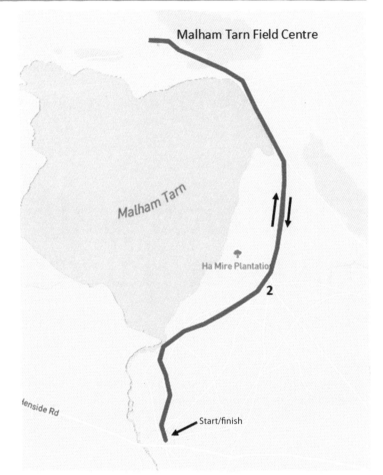

Malham Tarn Field Centre

Malham Tarn

Ha Mire Plantation

2

Ienside Rd

Start/finish

THINGS TO SEE AND DO NEARBY

Malham village is a great base for a number of excellent walks, including the beautiful waterfall at **Janet's Foss**, dramatic **Gordale Scar** and the fascinating limestone pavement that tops the great scoop of **Malham Cove**, once a vast waterfall and now a rock climbing destination for the best sport climbers, a spectacle well worth a watch.

58

Fountains and follies at Hackfall

HACKFALL, NORTH YORKSHIRE

The magical, ancient woodland at Hackfall cloaks a steep river gorge near to Ripon in North Yorkshire. A Site of Special Scientific Interest where leafy trails thread through oak, beech, sycamore and lime trees, this is also a place of surprises. In the 18th century, the Aislabie family, who owned the land, built a series of weird and wonderful follies, glades, grottos, temples and waterfalls, which still stand hidden within the woodland. Many of the trees were felled for timber in the 1930s but the 18th-century limes remain and the combined efforts of the Woodland Trust and the Landmark Trust have, over the past 30 years, restored the place to its former glory.

There are several waymarked walks at Hackfall, ranging from 0.75 miles (1.2km) to 4.5 miles (7.2km) – leaflets are usually available at the car park – but really there's endless scope for exploring. If you make it as far as the pretty village of Grewelthorpe, across a couple of fields to the south of the woods, the community cafe is well worth a visit. It's family friendly and it's a wonderful experience to sit outside in the little walled garden in the sunshine. Our choice of route, 'Cascades and Follies', balances the walking needs of little legs with the opportunity to see several follies, and also to have a go at the pump-operated fountain on an island in the centre of Fountain Pond.

WALK DETAILS

Start/finish: Hackfall Woodland Trust Car Park, 0.5 miles (0.8km) north of Grewelthorpe village, Ripon, nearest postcode HG4 3BU; grid ref SE230775

Distance: 1.5 miles (2.4km)

Difficulty: 2/5

Public transport: A couple of buses a day link Ripon and Masham via Grewelthorpe

NORTH ENGLAND

149

DIRECTIONS

1 Leave the car park via the kissing gate and turn left, following the track downhill to Limehouse Field Gate. Turn right just before the gate, go up some steps, through another kissing gate and across a field along the top of the woodland until you can turn left into the woodland.

2 Follow the path steeply downhill to reach Fountain Pond and the Rustic Temple. Don't forget to have a go at operating the fountain.

3 Carry on past the Grotto and the Forty Foot Fall, then hop over the stream and head right, up the hill.

4 Bear left off the main path to reach Alum Spring, crossing the stepping stones by the weir. From here, you can make the out-and-back trip to explore Mowbray Castle. Returning to the main path at Alum Spring, head uphill past Kent's Seat to the next junction.

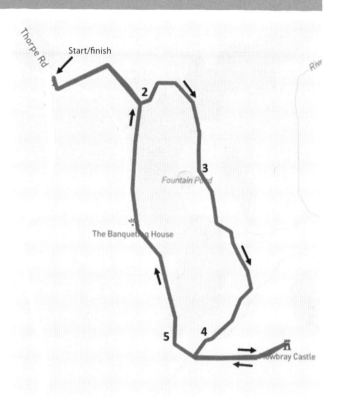

5 Turn right and follow the path to the viewpoint at The Ruin, carrying on along this path to return to the car park.

THINGS TO SEE AND DO NEARBY

Refuel with coffee and cake at the community cafe in **Grewelthorpe**.

Great places to explore nearby include the beautiful valley of **Nidderdale**, on the edge of the Yorkshire Dales National Park, **Brimham Rocks** (Walk 59) and the atmospheric ruins and wider estate at **Fountains Abbey** (National Trust membership/paid entry).

59

Roam round the rocks at Brimham

BRIMHAM, NORTH YORKSHIRE

Set within 400 acres of moorland, the sculpted, stacked rocks at Brimham make a wonderful natural playground. Stop for a picnic on the cropped grass, clamber around on the blocks or take in the views out across the surrounding Dales.

The rocks are made from Millstone Grit, a rough mixture of sand, grit, quartz and feldspar that was deposited here when the area was a vast river at the point where it met an ancient sea. Between 430 and 380 million years ago, a range of ancient mountains formed here as the modern-day continent of North America collided with Europe. Sand and grit would have washed off these mountains and mixed with other sediments over millions of years. Since its formation, the rocks have been eroded by water and weather into their fascinating shapes.

Many of the rocks have been named to reflect their shapes. There's a dancing bear, a rhino's head, a rabbit, a camel, an elephant's head and even a lizard's footprint, among others. This walk visits many of them, as well as taking in a loop of the wildlife-rich, tree-edged moorland and passing the oak tree that has been growing out of a rock for 250 years.

WALK DETAILS

Start/finish: Brimham Rocks, Summerbridge, Harrogate, HG3 4DW

Distance: 1.3 miles (2.1km)

Difficulty: 1/5

Public transport: Sunday service from Harrogate to Brimham Rocks, April to October, plus selected winter Sundays. Other services run from Harrogate to Pateley Bridge – alight Summerbridge, 2 miles (3.2km) from the start.

NORTH ENGLAND

DIRECTIONS

1 From the car park, take the sloping all-weather path behind the noticeboard and follow this through the rocks, passing Surprise View, from where there are beautiful views up Nidderdale.

2 From here, you can follow the main path around the edge of the rocks, exploring as you wish. The obvious loop is between 1–1.5 miles (1.6–2.4km) long, but younger children will be guided by their intrigue in the various rocks and the network of paths makes a perfect strolling ground for all.

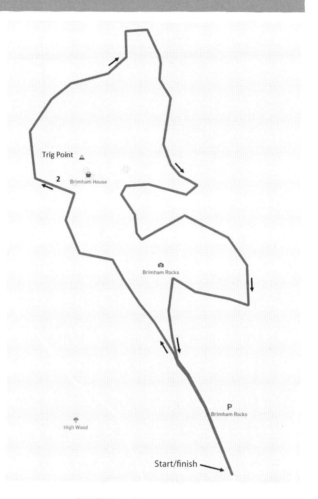

Trig Point ▲

2 Brimham House

📷 Brimham Rocks

P Brimham Rocks

High Wood

Start/finish

THINGS TO SEE AND DO NEARBY

Rock climbing is popular at **Brimham** and you can join organised groups to learn how to tackle some of the higher, steeper faces. There are also geocaching and orienteering courses on offer.

Further afield, **Nidderdale** is a beautiful, remote part of the Yorkshire Dales, networked with footpaths for exploration. This is a fantastic area for camping, with vast, dark skies for stargazing.

60

A surprise view from Otley Chevin

SOUTH PENNINES, WEST YORKSHIRE

The South Pennines lie hidden between their better-known neighbours, the Peak District and the Yorkshire Dales. This unique landscape has inspired many great writers and poets, including the Brontës and Ted Hughes. It is a vast, open area of sweeping high moorland intersected by steep-sided narrow valleys containing settlements built using the local gritstone. The hillsides and pastures bear the scars of a long history of human use, from Mesolithic, Bronze Age and Iron Age relics to Roman roads and hill forts and the mills and factories of the Industrial Revolution, powered by the area's fast-flowing streams.

The peaceful expanses of gritstone moorland feel wonderfully remote, and are covered in a network of trails, footpaths, bridleways and ancient packhorse roads that provide easy access to wild places and good year-round walking. The South Pennines Walk and Ride Festival is a fantastic annual event for those who enjoy exploring the great outdoors.

Otley Chevin is an imposing Millstone Grit edge, overlooking the town of Otley and the Wharfe Valley. The Chevin itself lies within the Chevin Forest Park, and despite being only 1 mile (1.6km) away from Leeds Bradford airport, there's a real feeling of adventure here. The highest point – Surprise View at 925 feet (282 metres) – is recognised as one of the finest viewpoints in Yorkshire, with views of up to 40 miles (60km) on a clear day.

WALK DETAILS

Start/finish: Surprise View Car Park at Otley Chevin (not the Surprise View Car Park in the Peak District!), Guiseley, Otley, LS21 3DG

Distance: 2.3 miles (3.7km)

Difficulty: 3/5

Public transport: A shuttle bus operates between the park and Otley bus station

DIRECTIONS

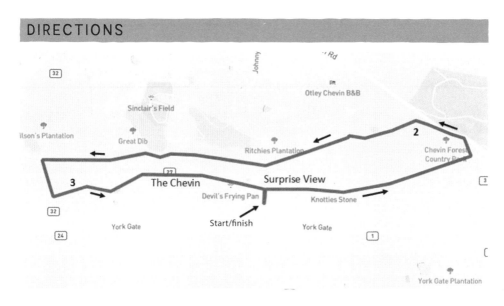

1. Turn right out of the car park and follow the path east until just before you reach East Chevin Road. Don't cross the road; instead, turn left and walk alongside it, down the hill and then left, heading west along a track running parallel to the one you started out on.

2. Follow the path through woodland for about 1 mile (1.6km). When the path ends, turn left and walk uphill towards Woodlands Farm, then left again, passing some scattered rocks – the remnants of past quarrying.

3. Follow this path eastwards, passing Yorkgate Quarry, to return to Surprise View.

THINGS TO SEE AND DO NEARBY

The wider forest park and neighbouring **Caley Deer Park** are all great for exploration. There are many excellent cycling routes and other interesting walks, including a nice little mini mountain to the trig point at the top of the deer park, as well as orienteering and geocaching. The cycling is particularly good on the eastern side of the Chevin.

   Caley Crags, also to the east of the Chevin, is a popular bouldering venue and a good spot from which to watch climbers tackling the various 'problems' up the rocks.

61

Follow the Vikings up Roseberry Topping

NORTH YORK MOORS, NORTH YORKSHIRE

Sometimes called Yorkshire's mini Matterhorn, Roseberry Topping, with its distinctive asymmetrical shape, is a well-known local landmark, rising from the edge of the North York Moors and visible from many miles around. Once a more regular sugarloaf shape, the jagged cliff on its western slope was carved by a landslip in 1912. This prominent hill has drawn people to it for millennia, and its first recorded name dates back to the Vikings; even today there's something about Roseberry Topping that inspires people to climb it, and it's a brilliant mini mountain for kids to conquer.

The shortest route to the top, from Newton-under-Roseberry, starts on a winding trail through Newton Wood, which is carpeted with bluebells in summer and where you can often spot deer. Emerging on to open hillside, you'll tackle the obvious steep track to the summit. The panoramic views are worth every moment of the climb. For a slightly longer walk, the route described opposite winds through open fields and peaceful woodland before taking you up and over Roseberry Topping. From here, it's downhill all the way home, starting with the steep northern flanks of the hill, wandering through Newton Wood and emerging to join Roseberry Lane to finish.

WALK DETAILS

Start/finish: Newton-under-Roseberry Car Park, Roseberry Lane, Newton-under-Roseberry, TS9 6QR

Distance: 3.1 miles (5km)

Difficulty: 4/5

Public transport: The walk can easily be started from Great Ayton train station, following the footpath up past Undercliffe to join the route

DIRECTIONS

1 From the car park, follow the footpath that runs alongside the main road with the road on your right (don't cross the road). Turn left just before the railway, continuing along the footpath.

2 Turn left and then bear right into Cliff Ridge Wood, following the footpath along the edge of the woodland. Bear left around Cliff Rigg Quarry, then run straight across fields, following the footpath to the summit of Roseberry Topping.

3 From the summit, continue in the same direction, following the footpath down the northern side of the hill. On reaching woodland at the base of the hill, turn left and follow the footpath, then bridleway, back to the car park.

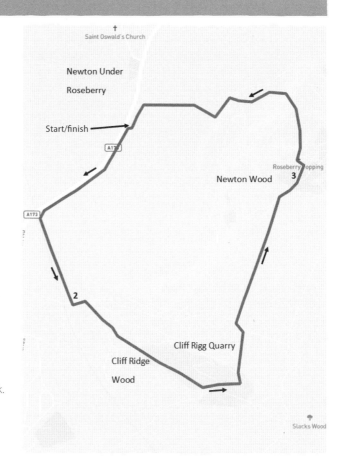

Saint Oswald's Church

Newton Under Roseberry

Start/finish

A173

A173

Newton Wood

Roseberry Topping

3

2

Cliff Rigg Quarry

Cliff Ridge Wood

Slacks Wood

THINGS TO SEE AND DO NEARBY

The coast from **Saltburn** to **Whitby** has many fascinating stretches, from **Warsett Hill**, another enjoyable walk, to the jumble of houses that meet at the harbour at **Staithes**. The small, sandy beach here is a great place for rock pooling and fossil hunting.

62

History and geology at the Hole of Horcum

NORTH YORK MOORS, NORTH YORKSHIRE

When driving from the coast at Whitby across the North York Moors towards Leeds, the view from the top of the Hole of Horcum is a truly awe-inspiring sight. It's a great place to stop and explore, either just to wander around the rim of the bowl or, as in the suggested walk, to follow the clear paths right down into its heart to discover a peaceful grassy valley.

As with so many geological wonders, there are myriad local legends explaining the formation of the Hole. The best known tells of Wade the Giant scooping up a huge handful of earth to hurl in anger. In reality, like the Devil's Punch Bowl in Surrey (Walk 27), the bowl was created by spring sapping, where underground water undermines the ground and, over millennia, the once-narrow valley widens and deepens into a bowl. Currently some 400 feet (123 metres) deep and nearly 1 mile (1.6km) wide, the process of gradual enlargement continues today.

If you're visiting with older children who are up for a longer walk, the full circuit of the Hole – taking in the wild and remote Levisham Moor on the opposite side – is a great walk of about 5 miles (8km). The track across the moor passes many fascinating archaeological remnants, including Bronze Age barrows, Iron Age boundary ditches, ancient enclosures and field systems. While this is an easy-to-follow walk on a clear, dry day, it's worth avoiding in very wet weather or when there's poor visibility.

WALK DETAILS

Start/finish: Parking area at Saltergate, just off the A169 opposite Hole of Horcum viewpoint; grid ref SE852936. Nearest post code YO18 7NR

Distance: 2 miles (3.2km)

Difficulty: 3/5

Public transport: Bus 840 Leeds to Whitby service stops at Saltergate, at the start of the walk

DIRECTIONS

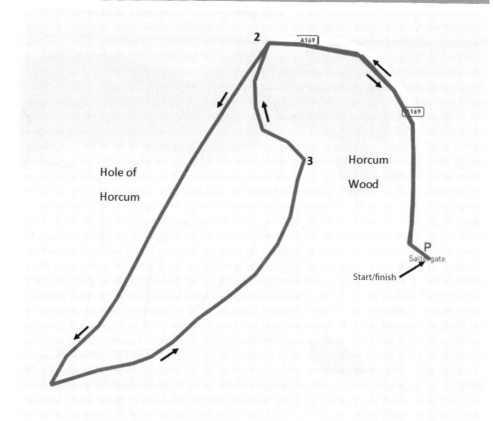

1 From the parking area, cross the A169 with caution to reach the viewpoint and footpath. Turn right and follow the footpath around the edge of the bowl, parallel to and below the road.

2 Where the road curves away to the right at a path junction, leave the main track, which continues across Levisham Moor, bearing left and then immediately right to follow an obvious path down into the bowl. You'll reach a path junction with an area of trees on your left once you reach the bottom; turn left here, around the trees, and follow the clear path back along the valley base, roughly parallel to your outward path.

3 As you near the end of the valley, take one of the smaller paths left to cut across to the upper path. Follow this back up and out of the Hole, turning right on to the main track once you reach the top to return to the start.

THINGS TO SEE AND DO NEARBY

A couple of miles to the south of the Hole of Horcum, the pretty village of **Levisham** makes a fantastic base for exploring the area. The **Horseshoe Inn** is a family-friendly pub that serves good food and also has rooms.

Levisham train station is on the **North York Moors Railway**, from where you can take a ride on a steam train, visiting **Goathland**, which starred as Hogsmeade Station in the 2001 film *Harry Potter and the Philosopher's Stone*. You can also walk to the Hole of Horcum direct from Levisham.

63

A waterfall walk through Eskdale

ESKDALE, CUMBRIA

Lying on the remote western edge of the Lake District, at the foot of the winding Hardknott Pass and the south-western flanks of Scafell, Eskdale remains relatively undiscovered yet is a perfect place for family adventures. The Ravenglass and Eskdale Railway connects the village of Boot, in the heart of Eskdale, with the coast using heritage steam engines. Built a little over 100 years ago, it's one of the oldest and longest narrow-gauge railways in England, known affectionately as 'La'al Ratty', meaning 'little railway' in old Cumbrian dialect. The line is 7 miles (11.3km) long – a 40-minute journey through spectacular scenery, which means you'll have plenty of time to explore Ravenglass before jumping back on the train for the return trip.

This walk takes you alongside the River Esk, which is dotted with spots for paddling over the warmer months, and with views across to the series of waterfalls that tumble off the higher fells. There's a good path either side of the river so an out-and-back amble works well for younger children. The full loop heads into the more rugged terrain on the opposite side of the valley, offering yet more adventurous walking.

WALK DETAILS

Start/finish: Dalegarth for Boot Rail Station, Eskdale, CA19 1TF

Distance: 3.5 miles (5.6km)

Difficulty: 4/5

Public transport: Train to Ravenglass then catch the La'al Ratty to Boot

DIRECTIONS

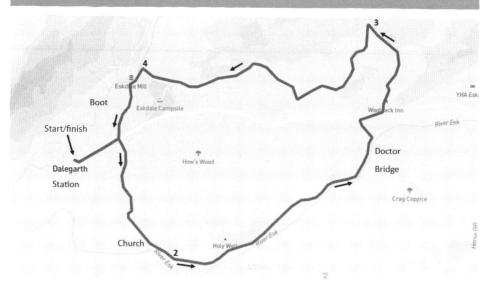

1 Turn left out of Dalegarth train station and follow the valley road 820 feet (250 metres) to a lane on the right. Turn right and follow the lane to St Catherine's Church beside the River Esk. Turn left here and follow the footpath alongside the river. You can cross the river over the footbridge at Gill Force to walk on the opposite side and make a shorter loop.

2 Continue along the riverside path until you reach the road just west of the Woolpack Inn. Turn right on to the road and then left at the Inn, following footpath signs to the left of the buildings and up into the fells.

3 At the junction, bear left, heading back towards the road, but at the next junction, where the left option would take you to the road, stay right and carry on past a house on your right. Bear left at the next house and follow the footpath along the top of the campsite to reach a bridleway.

4 Turn left and cross the bridge into Boot, passing the pub and carrying straight on until you reach a T-junction. Turn right here to return to the station.

THINGS TO SEE AND DO NEARBY

The campsite at Eskdale is excellent and very family friendly.

Jump on a steam train to **Ravenglass** or follow the winding lanes around to beautiful **Wasdale**. There's a cafe at **Dalegarth train station** and a decent, family- and dog-friendly pub, **The Woolpack**, at the halfway point of the walk.

Stanley Ghyll Force, a waterfall to the south of the valley, and **Eel Tarn** and **Blea Tarn**, both to the north, are all beautiful, peaceful places to visit and are within easy reach of Boot.

64

Ghylls and glaciers in Great Langdale

LANGDALE, CUMBRIA

Taking its name from the Old Norse for 'Long Valley', Langdale covers more than 12,000 acres of spectacular Lakeland landscape. A classic U-shaped glacial valley, Great Langdale snakes its way westwards from Ambleside, the mountains that rise either side growing higher and more rugged all the way. The head of the valley is ringed by the jagged tops of Bowfell, Crinkle Crags and the Langdale pikes, home to many classic walking, fell running and rock climbing challenges.

There are some fantastic adventures for littler legs here, too, including the scrambly path that climbs alongside Stickle Ghyll up to Stickle Tarn, and the mini summit of Side Pike, overlooking the National Trust's Great Langdale Campsite. There's plenty of history to be found, from the remnants of Neolithic stone axe making to the late Neolithic or Bronze Age rock art that can be seen on Langdale Boulders at Copt Howe near Chapel Stile.

This walk takes in a low-level loop of the valley, giving you plenty of time to admire the breathtaking scenery. Starting and finishing outside the Sticklebarn, a family-friendly National Trust-owned pub, it follows the Cumbria Way along the southern edge of the valley, climbing high stiles and passing plenty of the local Herdwick sheep on the way. The return trip follows a level trail through the grassy valley floor, tracing the meandering Langdale Beck all the way back to the pub.

WALK DETAILS

Start/finish: Stickle Ghyll National Trust Car Park, Great Langdale, LA22 9JU

Distance: 2.6 miles (4.2km)

Difficulty: 3/5

Public transport: Bus 516 connects Windermere (nearest train station) and Ambleside with Great Langdale

DIRECTIONS

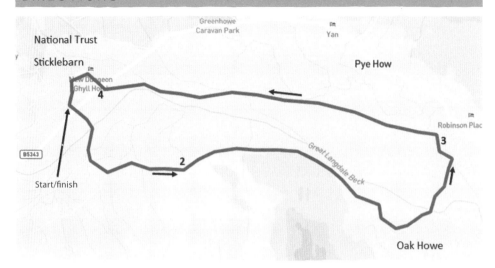

1. Leave the car park, walking downhill away from the Sticklebarn, and cross the road to the footpath opposite, which is also the Cumbria Way. Cross the stream and go through the gate by Side House, following the Cumbria Way up on to the open hillside.

2. Bear left, staying on the Cumbria Way as it curves around the base of Lingmoor Fell to reach the houses at Oak Howe. Follow the main path around to the left here, then bear left, leaving the Cumbria Way and crossing the stream on a footbridge to join a surfaced path.

3. Follow the path until it crosses a ditch, then turn left on a minor path, crossing to a larger surfaced path that runs back down the valley with the stream on its left. Turn left on to this and follow it until it brings you to the main road.

4. Cross the road to return to the New Dungeon Ghyll Hotel, Sticklebarn and car park.

THINGS TO SEE AND DO NEARBY

Camp at the National Trust's **Great Langdale Campsite**, waking up to fresh croissants and incredible mountain views. There's a family field with a play area in the centre.

Follow the **Cumbria Way** into the remote reaches of **Mickleden**, which branches off Great Langdale. The little stream is fun to play in and it's wonderfully peaceful and completely car-free.

65

Zigzag up the terraces at Loughrigg Fell

GRASMERE, CUMBRIA

The pretty village of Grasmere is an ideal base for a range of outdoor adventures, with excellent paddling and wild swimming in the lakes at both Grasmere itself and quieter Rydal Water nearby. Access to the surrounding mountains is also superb, with Fairfield, Helvellyn and the Langdale pikes within easy reach – although these are all bigger challenges. A walk up Sourmilk Ghyll, just north of Grasmere, brings you to Easedale Tarn, a perfect spot for a picnic and much gentler to climb, yet still with the same dramatic mountain scenery.

Overlooking both Grasmere and Rydal, Loughrigg Fell is a perfect mini mountain with a good path to the top that follows Loughrigg Terrace as it zigzags appealingly up its rough flanks. The wide, flat summit of the fell is both achievable yet very rewarding; it's only 1,165 feet (335 metres) high but it dominates the entrance to the Langdale Valley, standing proud at the end of the long ridge from High Raise. The views from the top on a clear day are outstanding: south to Windermere, west to Coniston and beyond to the Langdale Pikes.

There are many paths leading to the top of Loughrigg, and these make for some good exploring with older children. They include atmospheric Rydal Cave, just along the bridleway on the northern side of the fell. This walk is a great way to get started, taking you through woodland

WALK DETAILS

Start/finish: White Moss Car Park between Grasmere and Rydal, Ambleside, LA22 9SE

Distance: 3.7 miles (6km)

Difficulty: 4/5

Public transport: Regular buses between Rydal and Grasmere, stopping at White Moss and then following the most straightforward route to the top before you retrace your steps back down. Although this is one of the easier fells in the Lake District, it's still exposed at the top so, unless you're confident in your hill skills, it's worth saving it for a good-weather day, when you'll also get the best views.

DIRECTIONS

1 From the car park, follow the main path to reach the River Rothay (you'll need to cross the road if you park on the northern side; take care). Follow the riverside path with the water on your left until you reach a footbridge. Cross this and then follow the path through woodland with the river on your right.

2 When the path reaches Grasmere, just before the beach area, take a sharp left and follow the main path to a path junction. Turn sharp right here and follow the path along Loughrigg Terrace towards the trees.

3 Zigzag left before the trees and follow the main path steeply up to the trig point at the summit of Loughrigg Fell.

4 Retrace your outward route back down, taking in the glorious views as you go.

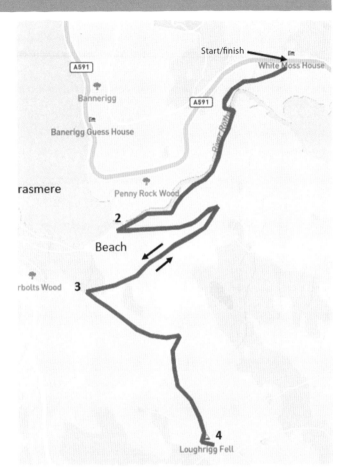

THINGS TO SEE AND DO NEARBY

There's a lovely paddling and swimming area on the southern shore of **Grasmere** – it can get busy but is wonderful at quieter times.

Grasmere village is fun to explore, with lots of family-friendly cafes.

The National Trust's **Allan Bank** – a Grade II listed villa – is a 10-minute walk from the centre of Grasmere and offers lots of activities for children. It's the ideal location for a picnic and watching red squirrels (National Trust membership/paid entry).

66

A hidden world at Tarn Hows

AMBLESIDE, CUMBRIA

Nestled in a low-level valley between Hawkshead and Coniston, Tarn Hows is quite unlike anywhere else in the Lake District. Easily accessible and with an even surfaced trail all the way around, the wild and mountainous backdrop gives the place a wonderfully adventurous feel with endless opportunities for exploring.

Back in the 1860s, Tarn Hows would have looked very different. It was originally three separate natural lakes set within a rugged lowland Lake District landscape. The estate owner at the time, James Garth Marshall, merged the tarns by damming the outflow to form one large ornamental lake and planted hundreds of non-native trees around it. In 1929, to protect it from development, the land was bought by Beatrix Potter – a passionate naturalist and Lake District resident as well as famous children's author. The estate is now managed by the National Trust, using traditional techniques and conservation grazing with Belted Galloway cattle to preserve the unique and fragile habitats.

This walk follows the gently undulating surfaced trail on a circumnavigation of the tarn. Cycling is not permitted, meaning it is especially safe for toddlers. Look out for red squirrels and circling birds of prey as you go.

WALK DETAILS

Start/finish: Tarn Hows National Trust Car Park, Ambleside, LA21 8AQ

Distance: 2 miles (3.2km)

Difficulty: 1/5

Public transport: Bus 505 from Hawkshead to Coniston stops at Hawkshead Hill Chapel, approximately 1 mile (1.6km) away. Follow road signs to Tarn Hows.

DIRECTIONS

1 Leave the car park, cross the road and bear left at the fork to follow the track down to the lakeside. Go through the gate and continue on the track in a clockwise direction around the Tarn.

2 You can either follow the main path all the way around the Tarn, which is the best option if you have a buggy or wheelchair with you, or take a slightly more off-road alternative route from about three-quarters of the way around. To follow this extension, bear left through a gate and up the hill to a high-level track. Follow this in the direction of Coniston and Hawkshead (signposted), taking in the great views as you go, back to the car park.

THINGS TO SEE AND DO NEARBY

Jump on a steam yacht gondola at **Coniston Pier** and explore Coniston from the water. You can stay on board for the full circuit or alight and walk across the fells back to the pier.

For Beatrix Potter fans, **Hill Top House**, where she wrote some of her best-loved stories, is well worth a visit and is fascinating for children to explore, spotting scenes from the books as you go.

NORTH ENGLAND

67

Conservation in action at Geltsdale

CASTLE CARROCK, CUMBRIA

As awareness of the impacts of climate change and biodiversity loss on the future of our planet – and ultimately our own species – increases, beacons of hope are lighting up across Britain, offering shining examples of better ways of doing things. Regeneration of degraded habitats through the co-operation of landowners, farmers and conservation organisations is restoring biodiversity to some wild places. Better management of landscapes is offering greater carbon sequestration, soil restoration and flooding reduction.

One of these inspiring places is Geltsdale, in the North Pennines, a remote and rugged landscape networked with footpaths and bridleways and scattered with the remnants of former settlements, quarries and lime kilns. The two hill farms, Geltsdale and Tarnhouse, together make up an RSPB Nature Reserve where conservation grazing, cutting rather than burning heather, and sensitive land management by local farmers are helping to restore the sphagnum bog, from which peat is formed. This wetland habitat is encouraging the return of wading birds such as lapwing, redshank and snipe. Greater biodiversity is also good news for birds of prey and if you're lucky you might spot rare hen harriers and barn owls hunting across the moors on this glorious walk.

WALK DETAILS

Start/finish: Parking area at Jockey Shield, 1 mile (1.6km) east of Castle Carrock village, CA8 9NF

Distance: 2.7 miles (4.3km)

Difficulty: 3/5

Public transport: Bus 680 infrequent service between Carlisle and Castle Carrock

NORTH ENGLAND

DIRECTIONS

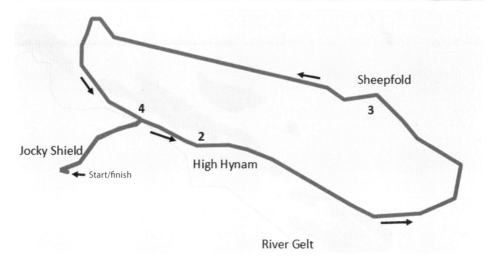

Sheepfold

3

4

Jocky Shield

2

← Start/finish

High Hynam

River Gelt

1 Turn right out of the parking area on the to lane and follow this briefly until you can turn right again, following a track downhill and across a bridge. Turn right immediately after the bridge and follow a bridleway alongside the peaceful River Gelt until you reach the houses at High Hynam. As a short out-and-back extension to this walk, you can continue following the river straight ahead here, passing some beautiful waterfalls and visiting the Gelt Boulder.

2 Bear left at the houses, continuing along the bridleway and following it uphill, steeply at first but gradually levelling out to glorious views across the surrounding North Pennines. At the path junction, bear left, following the wall, then left again, staying with the wall and passing a farm and some stone enclosures on your left. Continue until you reach a path junction with a wall straight ahead.

3 Turn left on to the obvious track and follow this downhill to reach an area of woodland. The track curves to the right and then to the left, going around the edge of the trees. Just after the left-hand bend, turn left on to a footpath running downhill through the wood to return to the River Gelt.

4 Turn right over the footbridge and retrace your steps back up to the lane and left to return to the parking area.

THINGS TO SEE AND DO NEARBY

The RSPB's waymarked walks around the **Geltsdale Nature Reserve** are easy to follow and enjoyable, with great opportunities to spot the local birdlife. The three walks of differing distances start from Clesketts Car Park (grid ref NY588584), near Hallbankgate.

Talkin Tarn Country Park, just north of Castle Carrock, is a great place for families to walk and explore, with a 65-acre glacial lake surrounded by 120 acres of woodland, fells and multi-use trails.

68

Discover a Roman fort at Hadrian's Wall

HALTWHISTLE, NORTHUMBERLAND

Hadrian's Wall is one of those parts of history we all hear about when we're studying the Romans. But actually standing next to this UNESCO World Heritage Site and seeing it winding across the rolling Northumbrian landscape is the only way to really appreciate the enormity of both the wall and the undertaking. Stretching 73 miles (117km) across northern England, marking the northernmost limits of the Roman province of Britannia, the Wall took six years and three legions of 15,000 men to build. It makes use of the natural Whin Sill dolerite escarpment, rising and falling with the rolling countryside – a true feat of engineering.

This walk follows an enjoyable circuit a short distance west of the famous Housesteads Roman Fort. Starting at Steel Rigg, with its high viewpoint, it visits peaceful Crag Lough and finishes along a stretch of the Hadrian's Wall National Trail, passing the much-photographed Sycamore Gap along the way.

WALK DETAILS

Start/finish: Steel Rigg Car Park, Henshaw, NE47 7AN

Distance: 3.4 miles (5.5km)

Difficulty: 4/5

Public transport: Nearest train station is Haltwhistle, 4 miles (6.4km) away. From here, catch the bus to Once brewed (Twice Brewed), 0.5 miles (0.8km) from the start of the walk.

DIRECTIONS

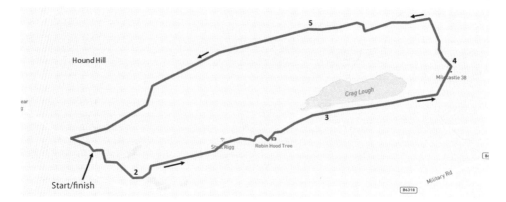

1 Leave the car park by the small gate in the corner, signposted 'Hadrian's Wall'. Follow the footpath until you reach the Wall, then turn left through a gate. Head down the hill, alongside the Wall, to reach a paved footpath at the bottom.

2 Turn left and follow the footpath steeply up to the top of Peel Crags, then follow the path alongside Hadrian's Wall to Milecastle 39 and then Sycamore Gap. Continue along the footpath as it skirts the top of Highshield Crags – caution: steep drop; a parallel lower path is an alternative that avoids the top of the crags.

3 Follow the path through a wood and over a stile, then take the next stile on your right. Cross the farm track and take the footpath through a gate signed to Housesteads. Carry on over a stile and past the farm on your left and through a gate, bearing right to a ladder stile.

4 Turn left immediately after the stile, climb over another stile, walk across a field and climb over a third stile. Continue following the footpath across a field, then turn right on to a farm track leading to a stile. Cross this and head across the next field to reach a barn.

5 Keeping the wall on your right, follow the path until it becomes a farm track and then a tarmac road. Turn left on to the road, following it up the hill and back to the car park.

THINGS TO SEE AND DO NEARBY

There's so much to see along this stretch of **Hadrian's Wall**, with plenty of opportunity to immerse yourself in real-life learning about the Romans. Visit the fascinating earth and stoneworks at milecastles 39A (**Peel Crag**) and 39B (**Steelrigg**). (Milecastles are small fortified gateways, built every Roman Mile, that may have protected weak points along the Wall.)

At **Housesteads Roman Fort** (English Heritage membership/paid entry) just to the east of Steel Rigg you can wander around the former barracks and hospital, and even see a Roman loo.

The **Sill National Landscape Discovery Centre** is near the start of this walk and is the place to find out more about the surrounding and wider areas. This sweeping, grass-roofed building also houses a shop, café and other facilities.

69

Ospreys and dark skies at Kielder

KIELDER, NORTHUMBERLAND

Holding some 44 billion gallons (200 billion litres) of water, Kielder boasts Britain's largest artificial lake by volume. Set within the remote and dramatic surroundings of Kielder Forest, this is a place where simply visiting feels like an adventure. Kielder Water's southern shore, along which the only road runs, is the more developed side, with visitor centres at Leaplish and Tower Knowe, camping, watersports, ferry trips and the osprey centre. The 26-mile (41.8km)-long, accessible lakeside way circumnavigates the lake and is popular with cyclists and walkers alike.

It is estimated that 85 per cent of Britons have never seen a truly dark sky, and Kielder is a perfect place in which to remedy this. Covering nearly 580 square miles (933 square km), Northumberland and Kielder Water and Forest International Dark Sky Park is the second largest area of protected night sky in Europe.

Kielder is also a fantastic place to see ospreys, which spend the warmer months in Britain, migrating to northern Africa for the winter. Having suffered a steep decline in numbers due to illegal killing, ospreys are now a protected species. Kielder Forest is the site of a successful breeding programme and you can spot the majestic birds hunting over the water between late March and early September. Peak hunting times are at dawn and dusk between June and August, when the birds catch fish for their young.

WALK DETAILS

Start/finish: Leaplish Waterside Park, Kielder, Hexham, NE48 1BT

Distance: 5.3 miles (8.5km)

Difficulty: 4/5

Public transport: Bus 694 runs one service daily, weekdays only, between Hexham and Kielder

This longer walk starts at Leaplish, near to the osprey centre, and then takes in an adventurous loop around the Bull Crag Peninsula. It's easy to shorten it should you wish, with an out-and-back to the viewpoint at Otterstone, which is all on good, smooth paths. The final section of the full walk, once you have left the lakeside way and crossed the peninsula towards the finish, is on rougher, more uneven trail.

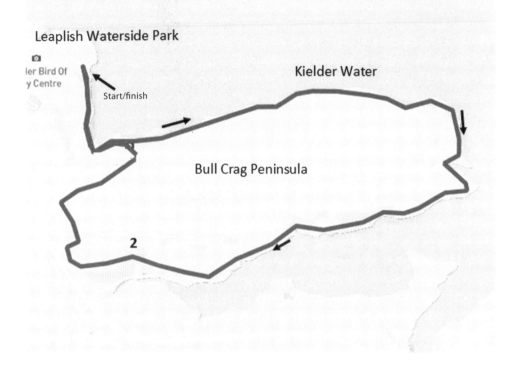

Leaplish Waterside Park

ler Bird Of
y Centre

Kielder Water

Start/finish

Bull Crag Peninsula

2

1 From Leaplish Waterside Park, follow the Lakeside Way towards the dam, with the water on your left. Follow this well-made path all the way around the peninsula, taking in the spectacular views out across the water. If you're visiting over the summer months, this is a great place to see ospreys hunting.

2 At the far end of the peninsula, where the Lakeside Way descends into the valley and crosses Cranecleugh Burn, keep straight ahead and follow the waymarked trail across the peninsula and back to Leaplish.

THINGS TO SEE AND DO NEARBY

Kielder Castle, managed by Forestry England, stands at the north-western end of Kielder Water. Explore around the castle and the Minotaur Maze, visit the observatory to learn about space (pre-booked tickets only), or head out on to the incredible network of walking and mountain biking trails.

NORTH ENGLAND

70

The lighthouse and the lost village at Souter

WHITBURN, SUNDERLAND

Standing proud on a grassy coastal headland midway between the rivers Tyne and Wear, Souter Lighthouse is an impressive sight from many miles around, its red and white stripes vibrant against a backdrop of sky and sea. Opened in 1871, Souter was the first lighthouse in the world to be powered by electricity.

This enjoyable walk traces inviting trails through coastal grasslands either side of the lighthouse, with fantastic coastal views from the limestone cliffs. The loop to the south explores Whitburn Coastal Park and Nature Reserve, once colliery land but since reclaimed to create a haven for wildlife. The northern loop takes in a large, flat field, popular with dog walkers and families.

It's hard to imagine that less than 70 years ago there was a bustling village on the site, housing the miners from nearby Whitburn Colliery. A combination of the closure of the colliery in 1968 and coastal erosion threatening buildings forced residents to move away and Marsden village was demolished, leaving no trace of its existence behind. The site is now looked after by the National Trust, and forms part of the Whitburn Coastal Park.

WALK DETAILS

Start/finish: Souter Lighthouse, Coast Road, Whitburn, SR6 7NH

Distance: 1.6 miles (2.6km)

Difficulty: 1/5

Public transport: Regular buses from South Shields

DIRECTIONS

1. Leave the car park and head south along the edge of Whitburn Coastal Park furthest from the sea. Continue until you reach the car park at its southern end, then follow the path around to the coastal edge of the park and walk along this until you reach the headland in front of Souter Lighthouse.

2. Continue straight on, following the coast path with the sea on your right and the grassy field to your left. Walk along the coast path until it curves left towards the road.

3. Turn left here and head back towards the lighthouse, crossing the grassy field and imagining the village that once stood here. Carry on to the lighthouse and back to the start.

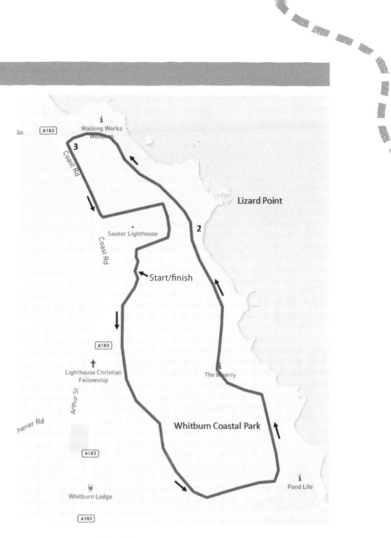

THINGS TO SEE AND DO NEARBY

To the north of Souter Lighthouse, the **Leas** is a 2.5-mile (4km) stretch of limestone cliffs, foreshore and coastal grassland. This area, including **Marsden Bay**, is a good place to spot seabirds; look out for kittiwakes, fulmars, cormorants, shags and guillemots, among others. Climb the 76 steps to the top of the lighthouse to admire the views and learn more of what the life of a lighthouse keeper would have been like (National Trust membership/paid entry). The cafe is free to enter, as is the seating and play area in the foghorn field.

71

Run around the ruins at Dunstanburgh

CRASTER, NORTHUMBERLAND

Setting out from the fishing village of Craster, the fragrant haze of the smokehouse filling the air – kippers are a local delicacy – there's an immense sense of excitement as the dark ruins of Dunstanburgh Castle come into view. Inviting paths stretch out across the sheep-cropped grass, edged by a rocky coastline and with the castle just close enough to feel achievable yet far enough away to be a real adventure to reach. Having such an inspiring goal to a walk helps if you're with reluctant walkers – and there's a hot chocolate waiting at the Stable Yard in Craster for the way back, too.

Standing proud on its remote headland, Dunstanburgh Castle was built between 1313 and 1322 by Earl Thomas of Lancaster as a show of his power. After Lancaster's execution in 1322, the castle passed to John of Gaunt, who strengthened it further against invasion from the Scots. During the Wars of the Roses in the mid-15th century, Dunstanburgh was captured twice by Yorkist forces before falling into ruin.

This walk takes on the classic trail across the coastal hillside from Craster. The castle is well worth exploring and free for National Trust and English Heritage members, but opening times are seasonal so check before you go. You can still get right up to the castle without going in, and a pleasant extension to the walk heads to its left as you approach, heading down through the dunes to the beautiful sandy beach at Embleton.

WALK DETAILS

Start/finish: Craster Car Park, Craster, Alnwick, NE66 3TT

Distance: 2.8 miles (4.5km)

Difficulty: 2/5

Public transport: X18 bus links train stations in Alnwick and Berwick with Craster

DIRECTIONS

1 Follow the footpath signs from the car park towards Craster village, heading down the steps to the harbour. Turn right to explore Craster and its smokehouse or left to begin the walk. Continue along the coast with the sea on your right, through the gate and across the grassy headland until you can bear right up the hill to reach the castle after about 1.3 miles (2.1km).

2 Explore the castle – it's well worth walking around its massive fortifications, even if you don't go in. To extend the walk, continue on your outbound path, keeping to the left of the castle and heading towards the sea. Bear right into some dunes edging a golf course and follow paths to drop down on to the beach at Embleton.

3 To return from the castle, either follow your outward path back or, for a slightly different route, bear right, heading up through the fields to join a parallel path inland that skirts the rough edges of the whinstone escarpment of The Heughs.

4 Bear left as you make your way back to Craster to return to the harbour, following the footpath back to the car park.

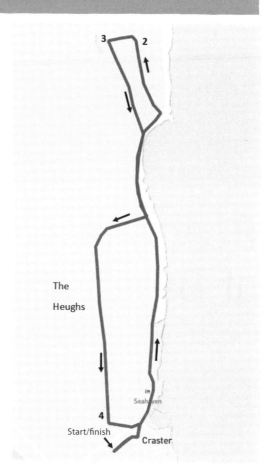

The Heughs

Seahaven

4

Start/finish

Craster

THINGS TO SEE AND DO NEARBY

The shop at the smokehouse in **Craster** sells traditionally oak-smoked kippers and salmon and other local food.

Heading north along the coast past Dunstanburgh Castle brings you to **Embleton Bay**, a good extension to the walk. Stick to the right of the golf course and down through the dunes to reach the beach. A great day out in its own right, the beach boasts a wide arc of sandy beach, peppered with rocky outcrops that gather intriguing pools and collections of seaweed, set against the dramatic backdrop of the castle.

72

Beaches and battles at Bamburgh

BAMBURGH, NORTHUMBERLAND

The magnificent outline of Bamburgh Castle, perched on its rocky outcrop looking out across Budle Bay towards Lindisfarne and the North Sea beyond, is a truly impressive sight. Unlike the romantic ruins of nearby Dunstanburgh Castle (see Walk 71), Bamburgh is imposingly complete, thanks to a £1m refurbishment by engineer Lord Armstrong in the late 19th century. The original castle dated back to the 6th century but was destroyed by the Vikings in 993CE. It was then rebuilt during the Norman Conquest, when it would have begun to look more as it does today. It's a fascinating place to explore inside – paid entry but under-4s go free.

This walk loops the castle, starting with a visit to the pretty village of Bamburgh before weaving through the high dunes and dropping down to wander along the vast stretch of sandy beach below. Look out towards the Farne Islands as you go – there are 15–20 of them, depending upon the tide. Over the summer months, they are home to more than 150,000 pairs of seabirds of over 23 different species, including puffins, kittiwakes, guillemots, black-headed gulls and terns, while in the autumn more than 1,000 grey seal pups are born here. Further to the west is Lindisfarne, linked to the mainland by a tidal causeway. Over the summer months, the beach at Bamburgh does get busy but come here in winter and, save for a few local dog walkers, you'll have acres of sand to yourselves.

WALK DETAILS

Start/finish: Bamburgh Beach Car Park, The Wynding, Bamburgh, NE69 7DD

Distance: 1.7 miles (2.7km)

Difficulty: 3/5

Public transport: X18 bus links train stations in Alnwick and Berwick with Bamburgh

DIRECTIONS

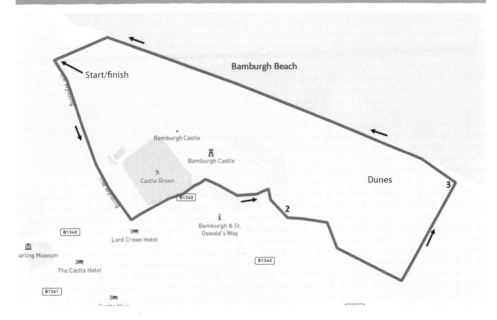

1 Turn left out of the car park and walk up The Wynding towards Bamburgh village. At the T-junction, turn left and follow the pavement around below the castle.

2 Walk as far as the castle car parks, just beyond the castle itself, then bear left, following sandy paths over the dunes and down on to the beach. To the right, the beach runs for 3 miles (4.8km) as far as neighbouring Seahouses, with some fascinating rocks to explore along the way. For the shortest walk, though, turn left and walk along the beach with the sea on your right.

3 Once you have walked past the castle, and just before you reach an inflow into the sea, head up left to a low point in the dunes to return to the car park.

THINGS TO SEE AND DO NEARBY

Bamburgh village has an excellent deli serving good picnic food, as well as the family- and dog-friendly Lobster Pot restaurant.

Budle Bay, just north-west of Bamburgh, is a haven for seabirds. The vast mudflats are home to geese, wigeon, teal, shelduck and mallard, along with waders including dunlin, redshank and ringed plover. You might also spot peregrines and merlins hunting along the coastal cliffs.

Lindisfarne also makes a great day out, with a ruined priory and a castle to explore and local seafood to sample. Check tide times before crossing the causeway.

WALES

73

A wild wander around Dinas Island

DINAS ISLAND, PEMBROKESHIRE

Bordered by the sea on three sides, Pembrokeshire, on the south-western tip of Wales, is home to the UK's only coastal National Park. It's a wild and beautiful place, edged by hidden coves and wide sandy beaches with an interior of wooded estuarine valleys, wildflower-filled grasslands and gentle waterways that flow through oak and ash woodland. The area is also a natural hub for adventure sport, including kayaking, swimming, surfing and rock climbing.

Jutting out from the north coast of Pembrokeshire, to the east of Fishguard Bay, Dinas Island is a wild and windswept place – a mixture of rolling farmland and rugged coast. It is not, in fact, an island – although it would take only a small rise in sea levels to make it one – but has a character all of its own, and a full circumnavigation of this tiny peninsula makes for a very special walk. Along the western coast you can watch the ferries going to and fro in the bay, linking this part of Wales with Rosslare in Ireland. There are glorious views from the trig point-topped summit of Pen-y-Fan and, at Needle Rock, you can see guillemots and many other sea birds in early summer.

There's incredible geology to discover, too, from the ancient, volcanic six-sided basalt columns of Pen Anglas – visible straight across Fishguard Bay from Dinas Island, to Pen-yr-Afr and Gernos, to the east. These are the highest cliffs in Pembrokeshire, formed from sandstone and mudstone laid down 450 million years ago.

WALK DETAILS

Start/finish: Pwllgwaelod Car Park, nearest postcode SA42 0SE; grid ref SN005398

Distance: 3 miles (4.8km)

Difficulty: 4/5

Public transport: The T5 bus links the train stations at Haverfordwest and Aberystwyth, stopping at Dinas Cross, 1 mile (1.6km) from the start of the walk

DIRECTIONS

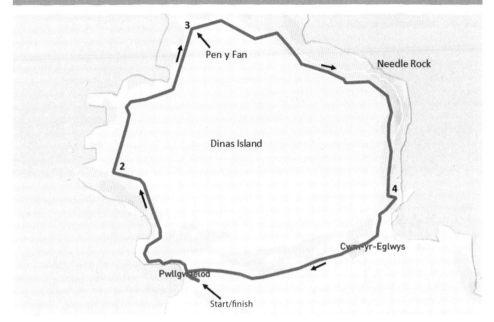

1. Turn right out of the car park, walking up the hill following 'Coast Path' signs. At the cattle grid, turn left through a kissing gate and follow the path up a section of hill with 40 steps, rewarded with beautiful views from the top.

2. Continue along the coast path, climbing up and over the highest point on Dinas Island, Pen-y-Fan, at 466 feet (142 metres) above sea level and marked with a trig point.

3. The walking is mostly downhill from now on, with some steep sections where younger children may need a hand. Follow the coast path through a kissing gate to reach a fork in the path. The left fork is the more rugged option, crossing some trickier terrain than the right-hand, inland path. The two paths reunite after a short distance, just before Cwm-yr-Eglwys Bay.

4. Continue following the coast path until you cross a timber footbridge to reach a road. Follow the road down to Cwm-yr-Eglwys and past the remains of the church, which was destroyed in a storm in 1859 that also wrecked 325 ships around the coast of Britain. Follow the path to the right of the boatyard, following signs to Pwllgwaelod through a car park and then through a valley on a surfaced path to return to your start point.

THINGS TO SEE AND DO NEARBY

Dinas Island is a wonderfully peaceful place to stay, with a campsite and holiday cottages to choose from.

Further afield, the **Treginnis Peninsula** and the **Marloes Peninsula**, on the far west of Pembrokeshire, offer many outstanding walks with stunning coastal views and wildlife. From Marloes, you can catch a ferry to **Skomer Island**, just less than 1 mile (1.6km) off the mainland coast and managed by the Wildlife Trust of South and West Wales. Famous for its puffins, you can also spot other seabirds, such as Manx shearwaters, razorbills, gannets and fulmars, as well as dolphins, harbour porpoises and Atlantic grey seals. There are regular day trips or you can even stay overnight on the island.

WALES

74

On the woodland trail at Pembrey

PEMBREY, CARMARTHENSHIRE

Nestled on the coast of South Wales between Gower and Pembrokeshire, Pembrey Country Park covers 500 acres of woodland and open spaces, perfect for exploring on foot or by bike. Many of the paths are accessible. There's a wealth of organised activities, from horse riding and archery to tobogganing and even dry slope skiing, but also plenty of wilder alternatives, from paddling and sandcastling on the 8-mile (12.9km) sandy beach to exploring the woods and parkland. Here, you'll find three differently themed waymarked trails – ideal for combining a walk with easy navigation – and there are plenty of opportunities to learn about the trees, ponds and plants you'll pass along the way.

Before it became a park, Pembrey was the site of an ordnance factory, with ammunition testing carried out in the safety of the sand dunes. Exploring this peaceful area today – or even in the height of summer when the beach is alive with the happy sound of families enjoying themselves – it's hard to imagine its explosive past.

This walk follows the Woodland Trail, leading you through a wide variety of different trees; look for Corsican pines, oak, willow, hazel, holly and sweet chestnut. In summer you might also see tiny butterflies – the dingy skipper, grizzled skipper and small blue. There are several bird hides around the park, too; watch for sparrowhawks, woodpeckers, blue tits, great tits, coal tits, dunnocks, chaffinches and more.

WALK DETAILS

Start/finish: Beach Entrance Car Park, Pembrey Country Park, Pembrey, SA16 0EJ

Distance: 1.9 miles (3.1km)

Difficulty: 1/5

Public transport: X11 bus connects Swansea with Carmarthen, stopping at Pembrey

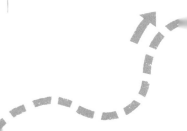

DIRECTIONS

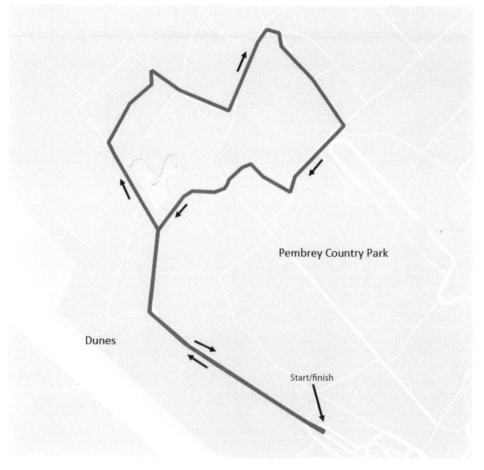

Pembrey Country Park

Dunes

Start/finish

1 The Woodland Trail begins at the Beach Entrance Car Park, following an easy-to-spot route around the woods.

THINGS TO SEE AND DO NEARBY

There's a lot to explore around the park, including other waymarked walks, cycling, horse riding and even skiing, as well as a campsite.

Further afield, explore the beautiful **Gower Area of Outstanding Natural Beauty** to the south (Walk 75) and **Pembrokeshire Coast National Park** to the north (Walk 73).

75

Discover a wreck at Rhossili

RHOSSILI, GOWER

The Gower Peninsula covers some 70 picturesque square miles of South Wales coast and countryside, designated in 1956 as the UK's first Area of Outstanding Natural Beauty. The peninsula's wildlife-rich countryside and lengthy coastline is dotted with nature reserves and ancient ruins and caves, where the remnants of millennia of human and animal habitation can be found, including fossilised mammoths and bears and the oldest cave art in Britain, thought to be more than 16,000 years old.

Set along the far western edge of Gower, Rhossili Bay is a perfect 3-mile (5km) sweep of golden sand backed by rolling downland. Visit at low tide and you might spot the oak ribs of the wreck of the *Helvetia* rising from the sand. Carrying 500 tons of timber, the ship ran aground in a storm in 1887.

This walk begins at Rhossili village, where you'll also find an excellent family-friendly cafe, National Trust shop and visitor centre. It starts with a steady climb up the downs to The Beacon, the highest point on the peninsula, for great views out over the Bristol Channel to Lundy. Descending enjoyably from the downs brings you to the beach to walk along the sands all the way back to Rhossili village. Shorter alternatives include a simple circuit of the beach or a circumnavigation of the Rhossili Peninsula, which is about 3.5 miles (5.6km).

WALK DETAILS

Start/finish: Rhossili village centre, Swansea, SA3 1PR

Distance: 4 miles (6.4km)

Difficulty: 3/5

Public transport: Regular buses from Swansea

DIRECTIONS

1 Follow the road through the village, taking the footpath by the bus stop as it bears left past the church. At the track junction, turn left and continue until you reach a gate signed to Rhossili Down. Follow the main path as it climbs the hill towards the top of the downs.

2 Stay left, continuing to follow the main path along the ridge to reach the trig point-topped summit of The Beacon, the highest point on the Gower Peninsula. Continue following the path as it descends steeply towards Hillend Caravan & Camping Park.

3 Go through the site, past Eddy's Restaurant and turn left on to the beach, following it all the way back to Rhossili.

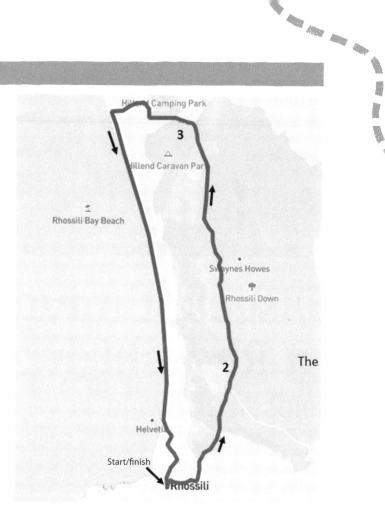

Hillend Camping Park
3
Hillend Caravan Park
Rhossili Bay Beach
Swaynes Howes
Rhossili Down
The
2
Helvetia
Start/finish
Rhossili

THINGS TO SEE AND DO NEARBY

Worm's Head, at the very end of the Rhossili Peninsula, is a jutting rocky promontory that's only accessible at low tide. It's a fun scramble with older, foot-sure children but can be tricky to cross and does get cut off by the tide.

South-east of Rhossili, **Oxwich Bay** and National Nature Reserve is fascinating to visit, with another golden stretch of beautiful sandy beach along with sand dunes, lakes, woods, cliffs and salt and freshwater marshland. Look out for wild orchids over the summer months, butterflies and other invertebrates, and a vast number of birds, including ducks, water rails, little grebes and moorhens. There are also two waymarked circular walks, perfect for spotting the reserve's wonderful wildlife.

76

A walk through waterfall country

BRECON BEACONS, POWYS

Nestled on the southern slopes of the Fforest Fawr massif, on the edge of the Brecon Beacons National Park, is Wales' waterfall country. This limestone landscape of lush wooded valleys cut through by fast-flowing rivers and undermined by a network of caves offers a world of truly absorbing, exciting walking. Along the Afon Mellte (River Mellte) and its tributaries, a series of spectacular falls fill the air with thunder and spray, many ending in deep, clear pools.

Just south of the village of Ystradfellte, the Afon Mellte disappears into the mouth of Porth-yr-Ogof (White Horse Cave), the largest cave entrance in Wales at nearly 66 feet (20 metres) wide and 10 feet (3 metres) high. The cave entrance is just a few minutes' walk from the car park down a steep climb on worn and uneven limestone, but worth it to peer into the vast network of caves and feel the icy blast of underground air. Henrhyd Falls, the highest waterfall in the Brecon Beacons, lying to the west of Ystradfellte, was used as the location for the Batcave in the 2012 film *The Dark Knight Rises*.

This beautiful walk follows the waymarked Four Falls Trail, visiting some of the most dramatic waterfalls near Ystradfellte. The route leads you through wooded gorges on paths that are often narrow and rocky, with steep drops and slippery surfaces – a real adventure best suited to those with sure feet. It's a very popular spot but absolutely magical, particularly if you are able to visit outside of the busiest times.

WALK DETAILS

Start/finish: Cwm Porth Car Park, Ystradfellte, Aberdare, CF44 9JF

Distance: 5 miles (8km)

Difficulty: 4/5

Public transport: Not easily reachable by public transport. Nearest train station is Aberdare.

DIRECTIONS

1 From the car park, follow the waymarked Four Falls Trail throughout. On the way, you will discover the waterfalls of Sgŵd Clun-Gwyn, Sgŵd Isaf Clun-Gwyn, Sgŵd-y-Pannwr and Sgŵd-yr-Eira on the River Mellte. The main path, marked with red arrows, is a well-maintained trail with gentle gradients and few steps, however the green waterfall link paths are rough, rocky and steep in places, suitable only for those with sure feet.

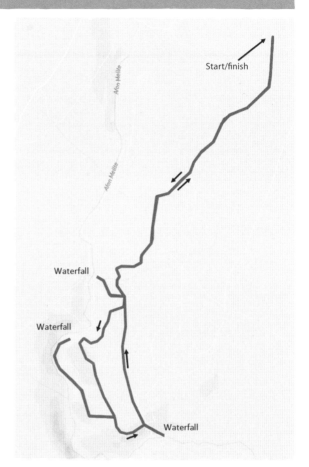

THINGS TO SEE AND DO NEARBY

There are several other waymarked trails to follow, all of which make a great walk: the **Elidir Trail** (1.3 miles/2.1km), the **Gunpowder Trail** (1.5 miles/2.4km), the **Sychryd Trail** (0.5 miles/0.8km) and the **Sgwd-yr-Eira Trail** (2 miles/3.2km).

Further to the north, the extensive mountains of the **Brecon Beacons** have endless opportunities for exploring, including Walk 77 and Walk 78 to the east in the Black Mountains.

77

Endless views on the Sugar Loaf

BLACK MOUNTAINS, MONMOUTHSHIRE

Flanked by sweeping grassy slopes and ancient oakwood valleys, the distinctive summit of the Sugar Loaf rises from the Black Mountains on the eastern edge of the Brecon Beacons National Park. At 1,955 feet (596 metres) above sea level, its summit is just short of being officially classified as a mountain. However, standing proud relative to its surroundings, it makes a fantastic viewpoint from which to see out across the Beacons to the summit of Pen-y-Fan to the west, the Usk Valley and the Bristol Channel in the south, and the rolling countryside of Herefordshire and Worcestershire to the east.

This straightforward yet hugely rewarding walk begins at the Llanwenarth National Trust Car Park. This is situated well over halfway from sea level to the summit already, and must be a contender for having the best car park views in the country. From here, it follows clear, inviting paths up the grassy hillside to reach a wild and rocky trig point-topped summit, standing on a beautiful long ridge. Make your way to the end furthest from the trig for a real feeling of wildness, particularly if you're there on a quiet day. From the summit, it's downhill all the way, back to the finish.

This is a great place to spot upland birds, from skylarks rising from the grassland and twittering high overhead to circling buzzards, red kites, fast-flying swallows and house martins, as well as red grouse. You might also see wild Welsh mountain ponies grazing on the hillside.

Start/finish: Llanwenarth National Trust Car Park, Abergavenny, NP7 7LA

Distance: 3.3 miles (5.3km)

Difficulty: 3/5

Public transport: Nearest train station is Abergavenny, 2 miles (3.2km) away. X43 bus service from Cardiff to Abergavenny and B4 Beacons Bus from Newport and Brecon stop on the A40.

DIRECTIONS

1 From the car park, turn left on to the surfaced road, then take one of the clear paths to the right, following this up the hillside until you reach the summit plateau of the Sugar Loaf. Aim for the trig point, from where you can explore the beautiful ridge and admire the views.

2 Turn around and head back the way you came, but bear right, following a parallel path back down the hillside to the car park.

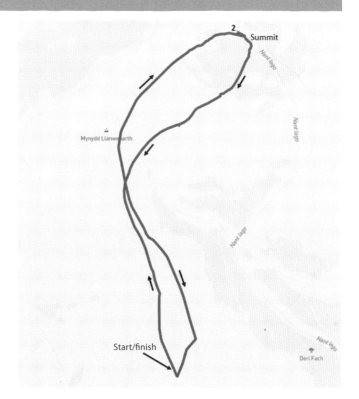

THINGS TO SEE AND DO NEARBY

The Sugar Loaf's two neighbouring summits, **Skirrid** (Walk 78) and **Blorenge**, also make excellent mini mountain summits.

The **Usk Valley** has many delightful spots, with peaceful sections of the river for paddling and swimming.

Abergavenny is well worth a visit and its market, open Tuesdays, Fridays and Saturdays, is fun to look around and a perfect place to find a picnic to take up into the hills.

78

Legends and landslips on the Skirrid

BRECON BEACONS, MONMOUTHSHIRE

Along the eastern edge of the Brecon Beacons, and forming the border between Wales and England, are the Black Mountains, a rolling range of slopes and ridges visible from far into Herefordshire. Here, the wedge-shaped hill of the Skirrid rises sharply from the surrounding lowlands, a striking mountain created by an Ice Age landslip. Its lower slopes are densely wooded, with a steeply winding trail that climbs through the trees before emerging on to breathtaking open mountainside. From here, an airy ridge leads you to the trig point-topped summit, from where there are fine views out across the Beacons landscape and the Usk Valley. The loop described overleaf is equally enjoyable in either direction.

A result of its sandstone geology, the shape of the Skirrid has been much determined by landslips over its history, including a large one that created the distinctive jagged outline of its north-western slope. Before its cause was known, however, the fact that the mountain looked as though it had been hewn in two (its Welsh name, Ysgyryd, means 'split' or 'shattered') was the subject of many a legend. Long considered a spiritual place, Skirrid is known locally as Holy Mountain on the grounds that it split at the moment of Christ's crucifixion. The medieval St Michael's Chapel, still part standing at the top of the hill, was used for services until the late 17th century. Another story is of an

WALK DETAILS

Start/finish: Car park at Llanddewi Skirrid, off B4521 Old Monmouth Road, Abergavenny, NP7 8AP

Distance: 3.1 miles (5km)

Difficulty: 4/5

Public transport: Trains to Abergavenny, 4 miles (6.4km) away

argument between the giant Jack O'Kent and the Devil over the height of their local hills. Jack stated that Sugar Loaf in the Black Mountains was the highest, while the Devil argued it was the Malvern Hills, just over the English border. On discovering that Jack was right, the Devil picked up a huge scoop of soil in his apron, intending to use it to add height to the Malverns. Unfortunately for the Devil, his apron strings snapped before he crossed the border, instead piling the soil at the northern end of the Skirrid.

DIRECTIONS

1 From the car park, take the gravel track and follow it around a sharp right bend. Continue into woodland and follow the obvious path uphill until you reach a wooden gate at the top of the woodland.

2 Continue straight ahead, emerging on to open hillside and following the obvious path up the main ridge of the hill to reach the trig point at its summit.

3 From here, you can either retrace your steps back down to the start or, for a slightly more challenging walk, continue as follows. From the summit, bear left and follow the footpath down the north-west of the hill, turning left as you reach a path that contours around the hill. Follow this path through the saddle and then through woodland to reach a path junction at the southern end of the hill.

4 At the path junction, continue straight ahead rather than going left uphill. Follow the path as it curves to the left around the end of the hill, eventually reaching a path junction with your outward route. Turn right here to descend back through the woods to the car park.

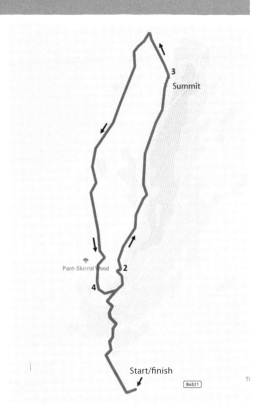

THINGS TO SEE AND DO NEARBY

Stretching across 500 square miles (800 square km) from south to mid-Wales, the **Brecon Beacons National Park** boasts some of the most spectacular and distinctive landscapes in southern Britain. The central Beacons dominate the skyline to the south of Brecon and rise to 2,907 feet (886 metres) at **Pen-y-Fan**, the highest point in south Wales. Further west lies the sandstone massif of **Fforest Fawr**, with its steep river valleys and spectacular waterfalls, and the imposing **Y Mynydd Du**, the Black Mountain range.

Wales' first **International Dark Sky Reserve**, the National Park is also a great place for stargazing; a weekend's camping here makes for a great adventure.

WALES

79

A foragers' walk on Hay Bluff

HAY BLUFF, POWYS

Hay Bluff stands at the northern end of the Black Mountains, an upland area of the eastern Brecon Beacons that straddles the Wales/England border. The bluff's distinctive slope, dropping off the end of the Hatterrall Ridge, is visible from far away across the Wye Valley and into Gloucestershire. A gentler, more approachable area than the central or western Beacons, the Black Mountains has a number of inviting summits and ridges that tend to be grassy and rolling – perfect for walks with younger children.

Hay Bluff rises above the pretty town of Hay-on-Wye, well known for its numerous bookshops and annual literary festival. The Offa's Dyke Path links the town and the Bluff and makes an excellent longer walk of around 8 miles (12.9km). For littler legs, however, the route described opposite takes in a short but exciting loop, where the terrain is steep but not too tricky.

Over the summer months, the top of Hatterrall Ridge is carpeted with bilberry bushes, perfect for some mid-walk foraging and a real delight for kids. These tiny wild blueberries grow in abundance on acidic, nutrient-poor soil on heaths, moors and some woodland right across Britain, but have different names depending upon where you find them: on Dartmoor, they're whortleberries; blaeberries in Scotland and the Lake District; hurtleberries in the south-east; and, elsewhere, whinberries, whimberries, windberries and myrtle berries.

WALK DETAILS

Start/finish: Parking area 0.6 miles (1km) north-east of HR3 5RJ and 0.6 miles (1km) north-west of Hay Bluff summit; grid ref SO239373

Distance: 2.6 miles (4.2km)

Difficulty: 3/5

Public transport: Buses to Hay-on-Wye, 3.1 miles (5km) from the start

DIRECTIONS

1 From the parking area, cross the road (with care) and take the path opposite, following this for a short distance until you reach a T-junction with the more obvious Offa's Dyke Path.

2 Turn right on to this and follow it in a south-easterly direction, ascending steeply to gain the top of the ridge. This is Hatterrall Ridge, and the Offa's Dyke Path runs along its top all the way to its southern end at Hatterrall Hill above the Vale of Ewyas.

3 At the path junction at the top of the ridge, turn sharp right, leaving the Offa's Dyke Path and heading north-west along the clear path to reach the trig point on Hay Bluff.

4 Facing in the same direction, take the left-hand path from the trig point, following this along the ridge briefly until you can turn right on a diagonal path down the hillside. Follow this path all the way back down to the road and parking area.

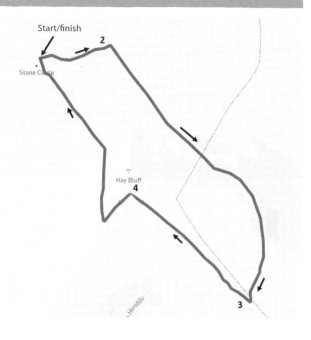

THINGS TO SEE AND DO NEARBY

Llanthony Priory, in the Vale of Ewyas at the southern end of the Hatterrall Ridge, is a beautiful, atmospheric, part-ruined priory set in spectacular mountain scenery. It's a wonderfully adventurous place to base yourself for a walk or a weekend, surrounded by a horseshoe of hills and with camping and a hotel on site.

Hay-on-Wye is also lovely to wander around, with plenty of good cafes, intriguing bookshops and long stretches of the River Wye, with shingle beaches for paddling.

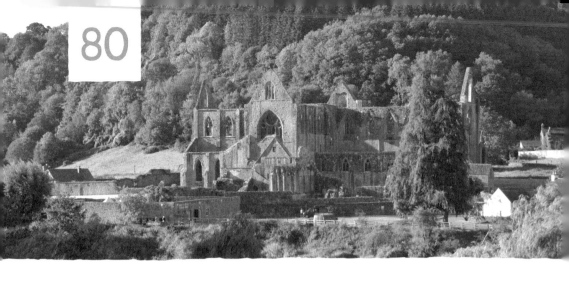

80

Walk with Wordsworth at Tintern Abbey

WYE VALLEY, MONMOUTHSHIRE

Set in a rugged, tree-lined stretch of the Wye Valley, on the banks of the meandering River Wye, the Cistercian abbey of Tintern is considered to be one of the greatest monastic ruins in Wales. It was founded in 1131 by Walter de Clare, Lord of Chepstow, and prospered from endowments of local land. Building at the site continued right up to its dissolution in 1536.

Today, the Abbey's majestic ruins rise ethereally from the valley, with light streaming through archways and windows and casting long, intricate shadows on the neatly clipped grass. You can wander in the grounds surrounding Tintern Abbey for free, but to explore inside you'll need Cadw membership or to purchase tickets.

Starting in front of the Abbey, this out-and-back walk heads along the western bank of the River Wye before crossing over the river and climbing on winding, woodland trails towards the Offa's Dyke Path. This takes you to the high point of the Devil's Pulpit, a limestone rock jutting out from the cliffs. Legend has it the Devil would preach to the monks below, tempting them to stray from their strict code of conduct. Taking in the magical views from the top it's easy to see how Wordsworth was inspired to write his poem *Lines Composed a Few Miles above Tintern Abbey* on his visit in 1798.

WALK DETAILS

Start/finish: Car park just off the A466 at Tintern Abbey, nearest postcode NP16 6SE

Distance: 3.1 miles (5km)

Difficulty: 4/5

Public transport: Nearest train station is at Chepstow. Regular bus service connects Monmouth and Chepstow via Tintern.

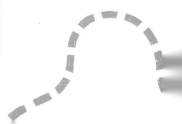

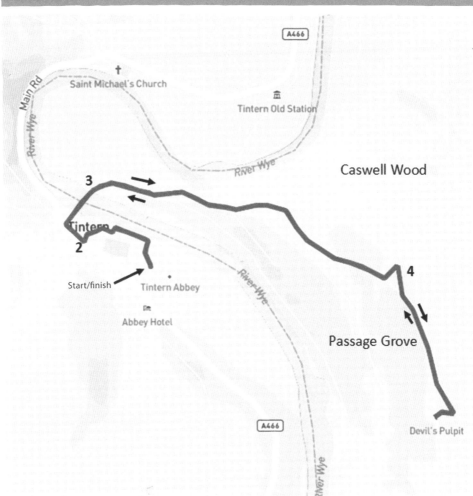

1. From the car park, follow the minor road towards the River Wye. Turn left at the mini roundabout and follow the path alongside the river and then around to the left past houses to reach the A466.

2. Turn right and walk along the pavement with care (caution: busy road) for a short distance until you can turn right on to a footpath that takes you over a footbridge, crossing the river.

3. Follow the footpath signed to the Offa's Dyke Path and Devil's Pulpit uphill through woodland, heading through the trees in an east and then south-easterly direction. Keep going uphill at junctions to reach the Offa's Dyke Path at the top. Caution: this path is steep, rocky and stepped in places.

4. Turn right on to the Offa's Dyke Path and follow this up to the Devil's Pulpit. Return by your outward route.

THINGS TO SEE AND DO NEARBY

The **River Wye** is excellent for canoeing, kayaking and paddleboarding and there are many good outdoor adventure companies offering hire, tuition and guided paddles.

The nearby **Forest of Dean** is a great place to walk and cycle. **Cannop Cycle Centre** offers trails for all ages and abilities, with bike hire available on site.

81

Giants and glaciers on Cadair Idris

DOLGELLAU, SOUTHERN SNOWDONIA

The myths and legends of Wales see many giants dwelling on its mountains and within its ancient castles. One such giant was Idris, who sat atop Cadair Idris in southern Snowdonia, gazing up at the stars in the vast skies from his great rock-hewn chair. The chair itself is said to inflict madness, poetic inspiration or death on those who sleep upon it.

The picture-perfect Cadair Idris rises in a peaceful part of Snowdonia, well away from the busier parts around Snowdon. There are three main tracks to the summit, of which the Pony Path is the most straightforward, although it's still a big day out with a lot of ascent and a high, exposed, weather-affected summit. For most families, the first section of the Minffordd Path, which leads up from the southern side of the mountain to Llyn Cau, is a good but manageable challenge.

The shores of the 'closed lake' in its glacial bowl, carved out during the last ice age, are perfect for a picnic. Look for the roches moutonnées (sheepback rocks) – teardrop-shaped hills also carved by glaciers – and the huge 'erratic' boulder at your finish point. This quartz block is of a different rock type entirely from the surrounding mountain, likely carried here, trapped in glacial ice, from far away.

Caution: the Minffordd Path is unmarked and quickly becomes steep and technical beyond Llyn Cau. If you wish to walk to the summit, the Pony Path from Ty-nant Car Park (LL40 1TN) is our suggested route.

WALK DETAILS

Start/finish: Dôl Idris Car Park at junction of A487 and B4405, nearest postcode LL36 9AJ

Distance: 3 miles (4.8km)

Difficulty: 5/5

Public transport: Bus services 30, 32, 34 (Dolgellau to Tywyn to Machynlleth) run on the A487, stopping at the junction with the B4405 close to the entrance of the car park

DIRECTIONS

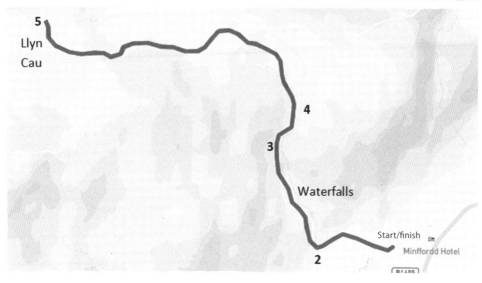

5 Llyn Cau

4

3

Waterfalls

Start/finish
Minffordd Hotel

2

1 Leave the car park through the gate beside the toilet block, turn right and follow the tree-lined track to a left bend. Continue on the track past an old cottage to reach a right turn on to a footpath.

2 Follow this path, signed to Cadair Idris, through a gate into woodland. Continue on the path steeply uphill using the stone and wooden steps with views of the waterfalls on the right. When the gradient starts to ease, follow the path to the right and over a small bridge and out on to the open mountainside.

3 Continue uphill on the surfaced path, roughly following the Nant Cadair stream on your right to reach a path junction and small slate bridge.

4 Don't cross the bridge. Instead, continue on the path as it moves away from the stream and curves to the left, heading uphill into the bowl of Cwm Cau. Follow the path up a grassy area and then on to a stony path, staying right here and continuing on the main path into the cwm. Carry on up, staying right, to reach the lake – Llyn Cau.

5 Return by the same route.

THINGS TO SEE AND DO NEARBY

Dôl Idris Nature Reserve, accessed from the car park at the start of the walk, is ideal for littler legs or if the weather isn't good enough to climb Cadair Idris. There are four enjoyable waymarked walks that explore the lake, parkland and gorge.

Cadair Idris Visitor Centre and Tea Room are a short walk on a level path from the car park.

WALES

82

The Cefndeuddwr Trail at Coed-y-Brenin

COED-Y-BRENIN, SNOWDONIA NATIONAL PARK

On the southern edge of Snowdonia, Coed-y-Brenin Forest Park covers 9,000 acres of woodland, the terrain a mixture of high, steep-sided hills and deep, rocky river valleys. Formed some 500 million years ago, these rocks with their deposits of copper and gold were once sought after for mining, and you'll still see people panning for gold in the water today.

Having made its name as the UK's first dedicated bike park in the 1990s, it's now managed by Natural Resources Wales for timber and recreation. There is a wealth of well-maintained walking trails winding through the forest, many of which are suitable for families and are also accessible. There are also excellent running and mountain biking trails – with something suitable for every ability – making it a superb place to visit for families of all ages. In summer, the forest floor is covered in bilberries – perfect for some on-the-go foraging.

Our choice of walk follows a level, accessible trail that climbs gently through the boulder-strewn forest to reach the viewpoint at Cefndeuddwr. Stop here to take in the peaceful atmosphere and beautiful scenery, with views out to the tops of Y Garn and the Rhinogydd mountains. It's a wonderful spot for a picnic, complete with a bench. The descent follows a wide forest road back to the visitor centre, the start point for many other walks and rides, where there's also a playground, quiz trail, bike hire and cafe.

WALK DETAILS

Start/finish: Coed-y-Brenin Visitor Centre, Dolgefeiliau, Dolgellau, LL40 2HZ

Distance: 1 mile (1.6km)

Difficulty: 1/5

Public transport: Trains run to Barmouth and Blaenau Ffestiniog. Bus numbers T2 (Dolgellau to Aberystwyth) and 35 (Blaenau Ffestiniog to Dolgellau) pass the entry road to the car park.

DIRECTIONS

1. This walk follows the brown arrows around the fully waymarked Cefndeuddwr Trail from the visitor centre. The trail is wide and well-surfaced, with no steps or stiles and a gradual climb up to the viewpoint at Cefndeuddwr. From here, it follows a forest road back to the start point.

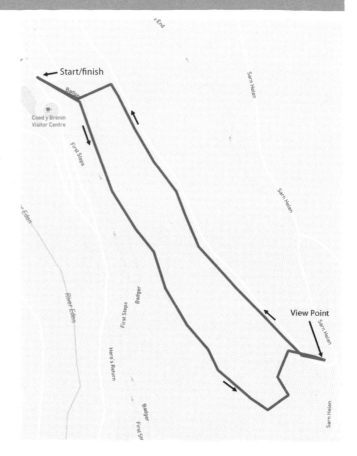

THINGS TO SEE AND DO NEARBY

There's lots more to explore in the forest at Coed-y-Brenin, but for something completely different, head to the beautiful sandy beach at nearby **Barmouth**. It's a popular spot in summer but with acres of space it rarely feels too busy. **Abermaw**, overlooking the beach, is good to explore, with a number of cafes and several walks heading out into the surrounding hills.

National Cycle Network Route 8 is a traffic-free trail from Barmouth to Dolgellau along the **Mawddach Estuary**.

83

Immersion in nature at Llyn Idwal

CWM IDWAL, SNOWDONIA NATIONAL PARK

Nestled at the meeting point of the great mountain ranges of the Carneddau and Glyderau, Cwm Idwal is Wales' oldest nature reserve. This is a dramatic yet peaceful place of rocky hillsides, cold, clear lakes – *llyns* in Welsh – and rare mountain wildlife encircled by high peaks. With more than 60 miles (96km) of paths, this is a popular place for walkers, fell runners and rock climbers. The National Trust's Ogwen Cottage Ranger Base and National Park centre at the heart of the valley is a great place to find out more about this fascinating area and how to explore it safely and enjoyably.

This walk is a great way to get started, winding up into the cwm from Ogwen and following an adventurous trail around the edge of the gleaming Llyn Idwal. As you walk, look out for hardy Welsh mountain ponies, feral goats, water voles and birds such as dotterel and peregrine falcons. Rare arctic alpine plants include the moss campion, Snowdon lily, alpine lady's-mantle and purple saxifrage.

There is also a wealth of archaeology here, with more than 1,000 known sites, including seven scheduled ancient monuments. In 2017, a team of rangers working on a footpath near Llyn Ogwen – which lies just to the north-east of Llyn Idwal and also makes a wonderful circular walk – discovered a sword buried in the ground. Experts date it the 6th century, around the time of King Arthur, supporting the local legend that Excalibur ended up in Llyn Ogwen.

WALK DETAILS

Start/finish: Ogwen Cottage, Nant Ffrancon, Bethesda, LL57 3LZ

Distance: 3 miles (4.8km)

Difficulty: 4/5

Public transport: Snowdon Sherpa buses run from Betws-y-Coed and Bangor to Ogwen Car Park. Pick-up available from Capel Curig and Bethesda.

WALES

DIRECTIONS

1 From the Ogwen Cottage Ranger Base, cross the bridge to the visitor centre and take the steps to the left. Go through the gate and over the wooden bridge, bearing right where the path forks to reach the lake shore.

2 Turn left and follow the path along the eastern shore of Llyn Idwal, climbing steadily to reach a junction with a path on the right. Straight ahead are the Idwal Slabs, which are popular with rock climbers.

3 Turn right and follow the path around the southern end of the lake, bearing right where another path joins from the left and continuing along the western shore and around the northern end of the lake.

4 Cross the slate footbridge and turn left, joining your outward path and following this back down to the Ogwen Cottage Ranger Base.

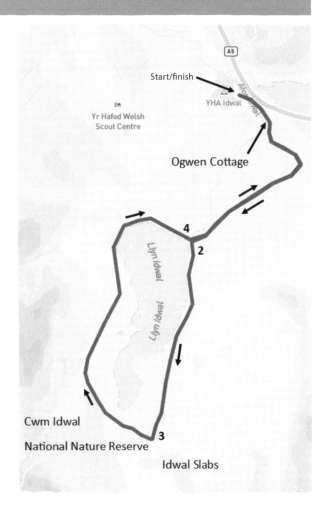

Start/finish

YHA Idwal

Yr Hafod Welsh Scout Centre

Ogwen Cottage

Llyn Idwal

Cwm Idwal
National Nature Reserve

Idwal Slabs

THINGS TO SEE AND DO NEARBY

There's a lot to explore in this part of Snowdonia, from a walk around **Llyn Ogwen**, to the north-east of Llyn Idwal, to camping near to the mighty mountain of **Tryfan**, just to the east. There's a campsite near to the foot of the mountain – a perfect adventure base from which to explore the area.

84

Dreaming of dolphins on the Llŷn Peninsula

LLŶN PENINSULA, GWYNEDD

The picturesque fishing villages of Morfa Nefyn and Porthdinllaen are set around the wide arc of the Porthdinllaen Bay on the Llŷn Peninsula in the far north-west of Wales. The peninsula stretches west from Snowdonia for 30 miles (48km) into the Irish Sea, surrounded by a spectacular coastline, and with a character all of its own.

There's an abundance of wonderful wildlife here, including a range of marine mammals, such as Atlantic grey seals, whales and porpoises. This part of the coast is also one of the best places to see dolphins in the country, with bottlenose, Risso's and Atlantic white-sided species all being visitors to the area. It is also a good place to see marine eelgrass, particularly in the area of water in front of Porthdinllaen village, where you may see it washed up on the shore. An important source of food and habitat for a range of sea life, it has sharply declined over the last few decades.

This walk starts in Morfa Nefyn and follows the sandy beach through Porthdinllaen, with its well-known beachside pub, the Ty Coch Inn – the 'Red House' in English – and on around the headland to discover Porthdinllaen Lifeboat Station, home to a Tamar class all-weather lifeboat. The station is open to visitors for a few hours each day and is fascinating to look around. From here, you can either head back along the beach or follow the inland route back to Morfa Nefyn. Caution: some sections may be affected by high tide.

WALK DETAILS

Start/finish: Morfa Nefyn Car Park, Gwynedd, nearest postcode LL53 6DB

Distance: 2.5 miles (4km)

Difficulty: 2/5

Public transport: The nearest train station is at Pwllheli, 15 miles (24km) away, from where the Pwllheli to Tudweiliog route goes to Morfa Nefyn.

DIRECTIONS

1 From the car park, follow the path down to the beach. Turn left and follow the sandy bay round, eventually reaching Porthdinllaen, and the distinctive red-painted pub, the Ty Coch Inn.

2 Follow the footpath past the information point at Caban Griff and over a rocky section, dotted with intriguing rock pools. Carry on up the hill, passing the lifeboat station and emerging on to a golf course.

3 From here, either return along the beach or follow the track across the golf course, past the clubhouse and through the car park, carrying on straight ahead until you reach the finish at Morfa Nefyn.

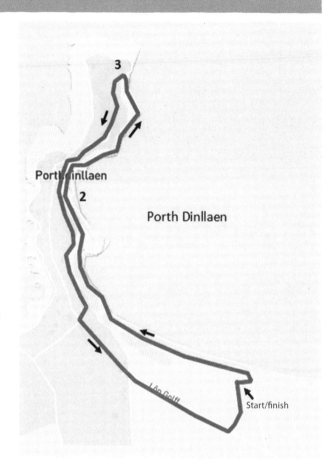

THINGS TO SEE AND DO NEARBY

The **Llŷn Peninsula** is an excellent place in which to base yourself for a few days of walking and adventures, with lots of campsites and holiday cottages to choose from.

Try paddleboarding at **Porthdinllaen** – a great way to see the eelgrass closer-up – or catch a ferry over to **Bardsey Island**, a fascinating place rich in history and wildlife 2 miles (3.2km) off the coast of the Llŷn Peninsula. You can even stay on the island.

WALES

85

A summit scramble on Holyhead Mountain

HOLYHEAD, ANGLESEY

The Isle of Anglesey lies over the Menai Strait from mainland Wales. With a long stretch of coastline and an abundance of wildlife, history and geology to discover, there's also lots of great family-friendly walking. As well as being a fantastic destination in its own right, Anglesey's coastal position means it's often sunny when dark clouds brood over neighbouring Snowdonia, making it an ideal place to escape to when the weather turns in the mountains.

Despite its name, Holyhead Mountain is not really a mountain at all; however, at 722 feet (220 metres), its summit is the highest point on Anglesey and definitely has a distinctly rocky, mountainous feeling about it. The rugged terrain and winding trails that cover the whole of this area make it fun for exploring, with wildlife-rich heathland and uninterrupted views out across the sea. The final stretch to the summit of Holyhead Mountain is a bit of a scramble, but nothing too tricky, and the views from the top are well worth the effort. On a clear day, you can see out across Gogarth Bay to the Wicklow Mountains in Ireland – and there's Caer-y-Twr hill fort to explore, too.

This enjoyable, varied walk takes you around Holyhead, from the imposing cliffs and RSPB Nature Reserve at South Stack, past the former fog signal station

WALK DETAILS

Start/finish: Car park on South Stack Road, Holyhead, LL65 1YH

Distance: 4.2 miles (6.8km)

Difficulty: 3/5

Public transport: Nearest train station is Holyhead, 1.9 miles (3km)

at North Stack and over the summit of Holyhead Mountain. The summit loop is best suited to older, sure-footed children and can be avoided by returning to South Stack on your outward path.

DIRECTIONS

1 Leave the car park and follow the clear path heading west towards the cliffs and Ellin's Tower and the Seabird Centre, standing within the RSPB reserve. Bear right as you join the coast path, following this with the sea to your left past South Stack, with its dramatically situated lighthouse.

2 Continue on the coast path northwards all the way to North Stack, staying on the main path at the top of the cliffs. There is a former fog signal station on the headland and fantastic views out across the rugged Anglesey coastline.

3 From North Stack, follow a path parallel to the coast path but a little inland, taking you across rugged heather moorland and eventually rejoining the coast path.

4 Bear left off the coast path when you reach the obvious path up the north-western side of Holyhead Mountain. Follow this up and over the summit and continue down the main path to the south, joining another path heading west as you reach the lower slopes, aiming for the radio masts and South Stack.

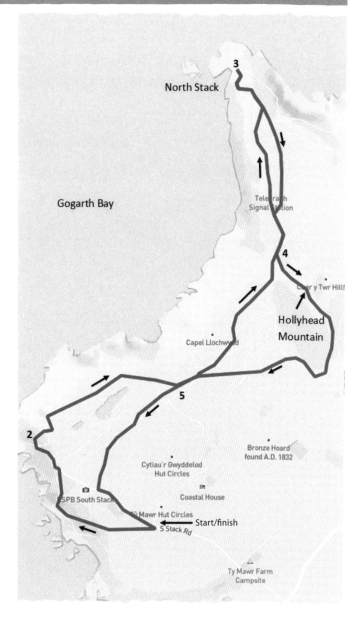

North Stack

Gogarth Bay

Telegraph Signal Station

Caer y Twr Hillf

Hollyhead Mountain

Capel Llochwyd

Bronze Hoard found A.D. 1832

Cytiau'r Gwyddelod Hut Circles

Coastal House

SPB South Stack

Mawr Hut Circles

S Stack Rd

Start/finish

Ty Mawr Farm Campsite

5 Bear left where you reach the coast path, following the path around to the Seabird Centre and then turning left again to return to the car park.

THINGS TO SEE AND DO NEARBY

The **RSPB South Stack Cliffs Nature Reserve** underwent extensive renovation in 2019 and has a shop, cafe and play area. There's lots to see and do, from guided walks and bird's-eye views from **Ellin's Tower** to three family-friendly nature trails.

86

Castles and canals at Llangollen

LLANGOLLEN, DENBIGHSHIRE

The small town of Llangollen lies in Denbighshire, in north-east Wales, and is surrounded by spectacular countryside offering a wealth of exciting places to explore. The winding River Dee makes its way through the heart of the town, flowing along the Vale of Llangollen and under the much-photographed Pontcysyllte Aqueduct, its 18 arches striding magnificently across the valley. Designed by Thomas Telford and William Jessop and completed in 1805, it channels the Llangollen Canal and its narrowboats, which glide improbably over the top. Since 2009, the aqueduct and 11-mile (17.7km) stretch of the canal has been designated a UNESCO World Heritage Site in recognition of its engineering ingenuity. Telford was also responsible for the nearby Horseshoe Falls, a weir of crescent-shaped steps that helps to create a pool of water to keep the canal levels constant.

This walk begins with a stretch along the canal, with views of the aqueduct in the distance. It then climbs up to explore the atmospheric ruins of the 13th-century Castell Dinas Brân, high on an outcrop overlooking the town, before dropping back to Llangollen. There are several options for parking in town, or you could arrive by steam train, on the Llangollen Railway. The walk begins at the bridge over the River Dee right in the centre, and next to the train station.

WALK DETAILS

Start/finish: Llangollen Bridge, Llangollen, LL20 8PG

Distance: 3.7 miles (6km)

Difficulty: 4/5

Public transport: Regular bus service Wrexham to Llangollen

WALES

DIRECTIONS

1 From the bridge, with the train station on your left, walk north to the T-junction, crossing the road at the pedestrian crossing and turning right alongside the A539. Take the first left on to Wharf Hill then, after a few yards, take the path on the right up to reach the Llangollen Canal towpath.

2 Follow the towpath east, with the water on your left, for just over 1 mile (1.6km) until you reach the first bridge over the canal at Llanddyn Cottage. Go over the bridge and follow the lane uphill, passing Llandyn Hall on your right and continuing until the entrance to Llandyn Hall Farm.

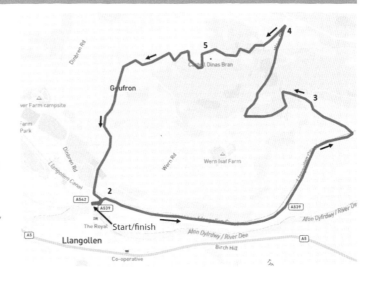

3 Turn left on to a footpath and follow this across fields, bearing left past Wern-uchaf to reach a lane. Turn right on to the lane and follow this uphill for about 0.5 miles (0.8km) until you reach a footpath signed to Castell Dinas Brân on the left.

4 Follow the footpath steeply uphill to the ruined 13th-century castle, taking some time to explore and admire the fantastic views out across Llangollen.

5 From the castle, continue in the same direction, descending west down the opposite side of the hill from the one you climbed to reach a fenced track. Follow this to a crossroads, going straight over here and following a narrow lane downhill to reach Wern Road. Carry straight on across the Llangollen Canal, continuing along Wharf Hill back to your start point.

THINGS TO SEE AND DO NEARBY

Take a ride on the heritage stream trains at **Llangollen Railway** (seasonal opening hours – check before visiting). Walk to nearby **Horseshoe Falls**, or dare to cross the **Pontcysyllte Aqueduct** on foot; there's a good path and railings all the way but it's best avoided by those without a good head for heights.

SCOTLAND

Dramatic discoveries in the Devil's Beef Tub

MOFFAT, DUMFRIES AND GALLOWAY

The Devil's Beef Tub, also known as the Marquis of Annandale's Beef-Tub, is a deep hollow in the hills north of the town of Moffat in the Scottish borders. Its unusual name is thought to derive from its historical use by the Border reivers – the Johnstone clan – as a place to hide stolen cattle. The reivers, or raiders, were often referred to as 'devils'.

The 500-foot (150-metre) bowl is surrounded by four steep-sided hills: Great Hill, Peat Knowe, Annanhead Hill and Ericstane Hill. 'It looks as if four hills were laying their heads together, to shut out daylight from the dark hollow space between them', says Sir Walter Scott in his novel *Redgauntlet*. But for all its chequered past and dark literary references, the Devil's Beef Tub is an enjoyable place to visit, filled with lush grasses and wildflowers and a peaceful, hidden place from which to admire the dramatic surroundings.

This walk follows the waymarked Devil's Beef Tub Walking Loop, set up by the Borders Forest Trust, which also owns Corehead Farm and the surrounding 1,580 acres, including the Beef Tub. It has regular, easy-to-spot red arrows and wooden footbridges to cross the boggiest parts – look out for dragonflies and marsh marigolds here in summer. While it does still get very muddy over the wetter months, this is an enjoyable, adventurous walk that kids will love to follow. Note: please park by the barn, just before the gate to the south of the main house and farm buildings at Corehead, rather than driving up to the farm itself.

WALK DETAILS

Start/finish: Corehead, Moffat, DG10 9LT; grid ref NT072122

Distance: 2.2 miles (3.5km)

Difficulty: 2/5

Public transport: Not easily reachable by public transport. The nearest town is Moffat, 4 miles (6.4km) from the start along the Annandale Way.

DIRECTIONS

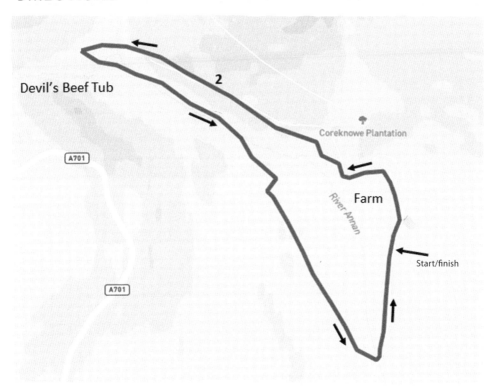

1 From Corehead Farm, follow the red waymarkers signed for the Devil's Beef Tub Walking Loop, taking you through the farmland and past a plantation, then cross rough grassland to reach the Beef Tub itself.

2 From the far end of the trail, the route follows the line of the wall to the right all the way back to reach the track south of the start – turn left to follow this back to Corehead.

THINGS TO SEE AND DO NEARBY

The Scottish Borders are wonderful walking country, with the **Lowther Hills** and **Southern Upland Way** both within easy reach of the Devil's Beef Tub. To the south-west of Moffat, **Dumfries** boasts the excellent **Kilnford Farm Shop**, where you can pick up picnic supplies while the kids explore the nature trail. Nearby **Dalbeattie Forest** has some good, family-friendly walking and cycling trails.

A circumambulation of St Abb's Head

ST ABBS, BERWICKSHIRE

The windswept headland at St Abbs lies just across the Anglo-Scottish border, on the north-east coast of Berwickshire. A place renowned for its wildlife, including vast seabird colonies and Atlantic grey seals, it has been a National Nature Reserve since 1984 and is looked after by the National Trust for Scotland. The precipitous cliffs along this stretch of the coastline are often obscured by fog. Following the sinking of the *Martello* on Carr Rock in 1857, the St Abb's Head Lighthouse was designed and built by brothers David and Thomas Stevenson in 1862. At the time, it would have had an oil-burning light but this was converted to an incandescent bulb in 1906 and, finally, to electricity in 1966.

This walk traces the coast path around St Abb's Head, starting in the north and exploring Mire Loch, the remains of St Abb's Nunnery, Kirk Hill and the lighthouse. The return stretch follows the intricate coastline, with spectacular views and plenty of birdlife to watch – look for guillemots, razorbills, puffins, kittiwakes, fulmars, shags and herring gulls, both gathering on the rocks and soaring over the waves in search of fish.

Combining a wild and remote feel with straightforward route-finding and a cafe at the finish, this is a thoroughly enjoyable walk and a great place to stop on your way north into Scotland. Caution: some of the clifftops are sheer and unfenced – please keep to paths and well away from the edges.

WALK DETAILS

Start/finish: St Abb's Head National Trust for Scotland Car Park, Northfield, Eyemouth, TD14 5QF; grid ref NT913674

Distance: 3.3 miles (5.3km)

Difficulty: 3/5

Public transport: Berwick-upon-Tweed train station is 14 miles (23km) away, then take bus 235 to St Abbs

SCOTLAND

DIRECTIONS

1 Turn right out of the car park and follow the lane north, passing the visitor centre on your right. Ignore the tracks that split off left from the lane, instead continuing to follow the lane, passing Mire Loch on your right, to reach the coast path at the northern end of the loch.

2 Turn right on to the coast path and follow it around the headland, making a loop around Mire Loch.

3 Continue following the coast path, heading south until you reach the B6438 at St Abbs. Turn right just before the road and follow the footpath back to the car park and visitor centre.

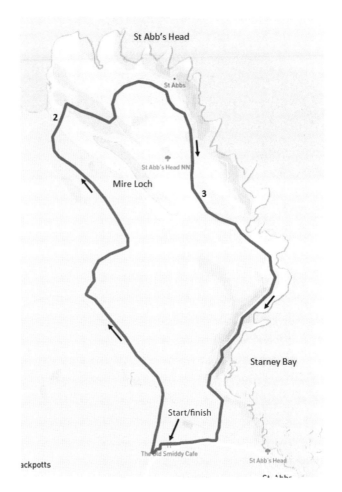

THINGS TO SEE AND DO NEARBY

The beautiful, sandy beaches at **Budle Bay** and **Bamburgh** (Walk 72) are a little way south along the coast from St Abbs, as well as imposing **Bamburgh Castle** and the fascinating castle and abbey on **Lindisfarne**, across a tidal causeway from the mainland. Hop on a boat from Seahouses to see the puffins and multitude of other seabirds around the Farne Islands.

Views and volcanoes on Arthur's Seat

EDINBURGH

Just a short walk from the bustling centre of Edinburgh, the 640-acre Holyrood Park is a wonderfully wild place in which to escape the city streets. Formerly a royal hunting estate, today the expanse of hills, lochs, cliffs and moorland are open to all.

The highest point of Holyrood Park is Arthur's Seat, an ancient volcano and 2,000-year-old hill fort that rises 823 feet (251 metres) above sea level. Visible from many miles around, the summit views are glorious; out across the city, the sea, the Pentland Hills and far beyond. Clear paths lead to the top, with varying degrees of difficulty, although all require a bit of a scramble to make the final couple of yards to the rocky summit pinnacle.

Arthur's Seat was formed by a series of volcanic eruptions more than 340 million years ago, with each eruption releasing more lava and raising the height of the hill. You'll walk over ancient lava flows on your ascent, while the summit would once have been concealed deep within the crater of a much higher volcano, eroded over millions of years.

There's something about climbing a volcano that kids really connect with, and it's a fantastic opportunity to learn more about the geological goings-on that shape the places we explore. There's more intriguing rock at Samson's Ribs, to the south of Arthur's Seat, where spectacular columnar basalt makes the craggy hillside look like a vast pipe organ.

WALK DETAILS

Start/finish: Scottish Parliament Building, Holyrood, Edinburgh, EH99 1SP

Distance: 2.5 miles (4km)

Difficulty: 3/5

Public transport: Short walk from main Edinburgh bus and train stops

DIRECTIONS

1 From the parking area at the front of the Scottish Parliament Building, cross Queen's Drive to reach the grass. There are two options for the ascent route: either follow the main path around under Salisbury Crags to avoid the most uneven ground or, if you're happy with rough ground, take the path that climbs up and along the top of the crags. Caution: sudden edges and steep drops near the top.

2 At the far end of Salisbury Crags, bear left to ascend the main zigzag stepped path to the top of Arthur's Seat. The main path skirts around to the right but it's well worth the scramble up to the trig point if you can, for fantastic views and that summit feeling.

3 Numerous paths lead off from the top in all directions, offering lots of possibilities for exploration, depending on how long a walk you want. A pleasant descent drops fairly steeply off the summit to the right, then takes the obvious path north along the ridge, bearing left just before St Margaret's Loch to descend towards Queen's Drive and the Parliament Building.

THINGS TO SEE AND DO NEARBY

There's lots more to do in **Holyrood Park**, including a visit to the 15th-century **St Anthony's Chapel** and walking to **Duddingston Loch** – a freshwater loch that's rich in birdlife.

Edinburgh offers a wealth of things to see and do for families of all ages, including a trip to the imposing **Edinburgh Castle**, high on the volcanic plug of Castle Rock. Nearby **Salisbury Crags** is the site of a revolutionary geological discovery; here, local geologist James Hutton found both sedimentary and igneous rocks, leading him to conclude they were formed by two different natural processes.

The mountain and the Maspie Den at Falkland and East Lomond

FALKLAND, FIFE

The pretty town of Falkland nestles between the two Lomonds – East Lomond and West Lomond – in the Howe of Fife. The Falkland Estate was once a hunting ground for Stuart royalty but today is a mixed landscape of upland pasture, farm and forest with many excellent walks for everyone to enjoy. The Lomond Hills are also a designated Regional Park – Scotland's first – assigned as such in 1986. Falkland is most famous for its fine Renaissance palace, inspired by the grand châteaux of France and once a favourite haunt of Mary, Queen of Scots. Looked after by the National Trust for Scotland, it boasts spectacular architecture, beautiful gardens and one of Britain's oldest tennis courts (paid entry/National Trust for Scotland membership).

This walk begins in the heart of Falkland, heading through woodland and up on to the open hillside of East Lomond, climbing steeply to the top for glorious views across the Fife countryside, to West Lomond and to the Forth Estuary. For a simple out-and-back walk, you can turn around and retrace your steps to Falkland. However, the second half of the walk is packed with fascinating features, including a rock-cut path that passes excitingly behind a waterfall and the Maspie Den – a network of paths laid out in the 19th century to showcase the Falkland Estate.

WALK DETAILS

Start/finish: Bruce Fountain, High Street, Falkland, KY15 7BU

Distance: 4.3 miles (7km)

Difficulty: 4/5

Public transport: Regular buses to Falkland from surrounding cities

SCOTLAND

DIRECTIONS

1 Starting at the Bruce Fountain in the centre of Falkland, walk up Cross Wynd, opposite the church, carrying on straight ahead out of the town. Continue on to a track, marked 'Private Road' and 'Footpath to East Lomond', staying right where the path forks.

2 Follow the path up some steps past the waterworks, continuing straight ahead and climbing through beech woods and a further flight of steps to reach the top of the woods.

[Map showing the route with numbered waypoints 1-8, locations including Tyndall Bruce Monument, Maspie Den, Temple of Decision, Start/finish, Falkland, East Lomond, and Craigmead car park]

3 Bear right, following the path across the slope and continue to the summit of East Lomond, crossing a stile and some steeper, rougher ground just before the top.

4 Descend by your outward route for the easier walk or, for the more adventurous second half, continue on the path south-west, descending a steep, stony section to reach a flatter, grassier path.

5 Continue following the path south-west, walking alongside a fence and then crossing the fence line to follow the track on the opposite side, eventually descending to a minor road opposite Craigmead Car Park. Cross and walk through the car park to the far corner to pick up a footpath signed to West Lomond.

6 Go through the gate and bear right, signed to Falkland, going through another gate and alongside woodland. Go through another gate and bear left at the next fork, crossing a footbridge and continuing through another gate.

7 After the gate, take the second path on the right, following this downhill to reach a waterfall. The path passes behind the waterfall; continue along the same side of the burn to reach the Maspie Den. Continue, crossing four wooden footbridges and then a stone one by a waterfall.

8 Carry straight on from here, ignoring the bridges to left and right until you reach a tunnel – it can get dark inside but it's not long. Emerging from the tunnel, pass under a bridge to reach the House of Falkland, then cross another bridge. Bear right on to a road, turning right and following this back into Falkland.

THINGS TO SEE AND DO NEARBY

Neighbouring **West Lomond** makes a great walk, starting in peaceful woodland and heading up on to open hillside to follow clear trails up to the trig point-topped summit for expansive views out across **Loch Leven** and the **Ochill Hills**. Stop off at the nearby **Pillars of Hercules** farm shop and café to stock up on picnic supplies.

A mountain adventure on Ben A'an

CALLANDER, PERTHSHIRE

Ben A'an is a picture perfect mini mountain, its pyramidal summit rising within the Trossachs between Loch Achray, Glen Finglas Reservoir and the long, shining stretch of Loch Katrine. While it only stands 1,490 feet (454 metres) above sea level, dwarfed by many of Scotland's mountain giants, it's an enjoyable climb with views from the top that rival those of many of the higher summits, really giving you the feel of a 'proper' climb.

This walk follows the recently upgraded path from its start point, just off the A821 and right on the shores of Loch Achray, to the top and back down the same route. It begins through trees, crossing and re-crossing a tumbling burn with views of that enticing pointed summit visible for much of the way. Emerging from the trees and making your way up the final open stretch of mountainside, the views await: along the length of Loch Katrine, to Ben Venue rising through the surrounding woodland, and over Loch Achray and part of Loch Venachar. To the west, you can spot Ben Lomond. At 3,196 feet (974 metres), it's more than twice as high as Ben A'an and sees more than 30,000 visitors to its summit each year.

Finding your way is straightforward and the path is good but there are several steep sections and, as with all high, exposed places, the weather conditions at the top can be much colder, windier and wetter than those at ground level so go prepared. In winter, Scotland's mountains require specialist skills and equipment.

WALK DETAILS

Start/finish: Ben A'an Car Park off the A821, Callander, FK17 8HY

Distance: 2.3 miles (3.7km)

Difficulty: 4/5

Public transport: Not easily reachable by public transport

SCOTLAND

DIRECTIONS

1 From the car park, cross the road and head up the obvious track, following this straight ahead through trees and crossing the burn, first over a footbridge and then a stepping stone.

2 There are several steep, rocky sections, including one heading around the back of the pointed summit of Ben A'an to gain the easy path to the top. Stay on this main path to the summit, admire the fantastic views, then return by the same route, with the views on show throughout.

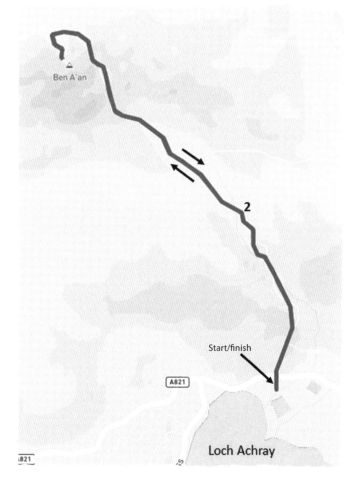

Ben A'an

2

Start/finish

A821

A821

Loch Achray

THINGS TO SEE AND DO NEARBY

There's plenty to explore in the surrounding **Loch Lomond & the Trossachs National Park**. Jump on the **SS *Sir Walter Scott*** steamship and explore **Loch Katrine** by boat; go mountain biking in **Queen Elizabeth Forest** park; or, if you enjoyed Ben A'an, try an ascent of one of the higher peaks of **Ben Venue** or **Ben Ledi** nearby.

On the Nature Trail at Ben Lawers

KILLIN, STIRLING

Cared for by the National Trust for Scotland, Ben Lawers is one of the country's highest Munros, reaching 3,984 feet (1,214 metres) at its summit and overlooking the serene waters of Loch Tay. The Ben Lawers National Nature Reserve at the foot of the mountain provides a wonderful natural adventure playground for children, where enticing paths wind through the rocky, wildlife-rich landscape dotted with intriguing archaeological remains. The reserve is home to the most celebrated collection of rare mountain plants in Britain and a staggering 600 different types of lichen, along with a vast number of creatures, such as red deer, ptarmigan, ring ouzels, skylarks and black grouse. If you're lucky, you might even spot rare viviparous lizards or wildcats.

This walk takes you on the waymarked, 1-mile (1.6km), family-friendly Edramucky Trail, which winds its way up the Edramucky Burn, crossing and re-crossing at intervals. It's an exciting adventure with a good amount of ascent and rough ground, in a beautiful, peaceful place with a backdrop of towering mountain tops, snow-capped for much of the year. On reaching the top of the waymarked trail, you can make an additional out-and-back to a group of ruined shielings – rough stone huts used by shepherds in the past – adding an extra 0.5 miles (0.8km) and a little more ascent to your walk.

WALK DETAILS

Start/finish: Ben Lawers National Trust for Scotland Car Park, Killin, FK21 8TY

Distance: 1 mile (1.6km)

Difficulty: 3/5

Public transport: Buses stop on the A827 road, from where it's a 1.6-mile (2.6km) uphill walk to the start

There's a range of other walking trails to suit all abilities, all of which start from the car park. Another excellent family-friendly route is the Kiltyrie Hidden History Trail, which is also 1 mile (1.6km) in length and takes in some of the fascinating sites of historical human habitation around the reserve.

DIRECTIONS

1 From the car park on the west side of the road, head through the walled area and follow the surfaced path through a gate. Cross the road, continuing to follow the path.

2 Enter the nature reserve through the gate in the protective deer fence, noting the change in the abundance of vegetation. This is the main path to ascend Ben Lawers. Instead, take the Edramucky Trail, which bears immediately right off this path and follows a smaller trail, crossing a footbridge over the burn.

3 Continue to follow the path, crossing the burn to the left for a while, then hopping across some stepping stones back to the right. Remember to stop and gaze back down at the beautiful views of Loch Tay.

4 Further up, you'll rejoin the main Ben Lawers path. Turning right here takes you up to the shielings, a few hundred yards further up. To continue on the Edramucky Trail, turn left and follow the main path downhill and across the burn, all the way back down to the visitor centre and car park.

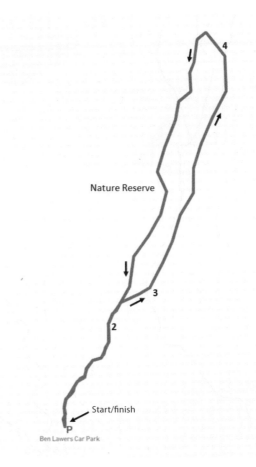

Nature Reserve

Start/finish

P
Ben Lawers Car Park

THINGS TO SEE AND DO NEARBY

In good weather, and with older children, the full ascent to the summit of **Ben Lawers** makes an excellent first Munro, with a good bit of height already gained by the time you reach the car park. Please bear in mind that the summit is very high and exposed, requiring good preparation, footwear and warm clothing. Poor-weather ascents should definitely be avoided.

    Loch Tay is great for exploring by kayak or paddleboard. **Killin Outdoor Centre**, at the western end of the loch, is a fantastic source of information and expertise and has kayaks for hire.

A poetic walk at the Birks of Aberfeldy

ABERFELDY, PERTHSHIRE

The beautiful wooded gorge of the Moness Burn, just outside the village of Aberfeldy, was once known as the Dens of Moness. However, the area was renamed in honour of Robert Burns' poem *The Birks o'Aberfeldie*, penned by the national bard in 1787 after he enjoyed a visit here. You'll find a few lines of the poem, and a life-sized statue of Burns, as you explore. It's a perfect place for an adventure, with winding paths and steps leading around a densely wooded, rocky ravine, through which tumbles a series of falls, filling the air with spray and thunder. From the very top, the Falls of Moness drop majestically in an 82 foot- (25 metre)-high waterfall.

Although 'birks' is Scottish for birch trees, the woods are actually a fine mixture of oak, birch, hazel and ash trees with a scattering of pine, and predominantly beech around the lower slopes. During the autumn, these are ablaze with leaves of orange, red and yellow. It is thought that the gorge has been continuously covered in woodland for some 8,000 years, and today it's designated a Site of Special Scientific Interest for its flora.

This walk follows the clear path on an adventurous journey up through the trees to reach the viewpoint at the very top. From the bridge here there are outstanding views down the gorge and the Tay valley to the mountains beyond and a real feeling of being high in the tree canopy.

WALK DETAILS

Start/finish: Upper Birks Car Park, Aberfeldy, PH15 2DX; grid ref NN855486 or follow signs from central Aberfeldy

Distance: 2.3 miles (3.7km)

Difficulty: 3/5

Public transport: Regular bus service to Aberfeldy

SCOTLAND

This is a great place to spot red squirrels, peering out from the boughs.

And, finally, a line from Burns' poem 'The Birks o'Aberfeldie':

> 'The braes ascend like
> lofty wa's,
> The foaming stream deep-roaring fa's,
> O'erhung wi' fragrant
> spreading shaws,
> The Birks o'Aberfeldie

(Note: 'wa's' are walls and 'fa's' are falls.)

DIRECTIONS

1 From the car park, follow the obvious trail, bearing left to cross the bridge over the Moness Burn. Follow the main path through woodland – the trees here are mainly beech – passing a series of small waterfalls.

2 Continue along the path, crossing the footbridge over a minor stream and passing a rocky area known as Burns' Seat – this was where the lines of the poem are said to have come to the poet. Follow the path up a steep section with zigzags and steps, passing some captivating waterfalls as you go, to reach a wooden walkway. At the end of this, the path forks – take the path to the left and admire the breathtaking views across the gorge.

3 Continue up to the top of the gorge, where a bridge over the Upper Moness Falls offers an incredible viewpoint down to the river.

4 Once over the bridge, turn right to follow the path down the opposite side of the river, winding through beautiful woodland with occasional glimpses of fine mountain views. This path eventually brings you back to the car park.

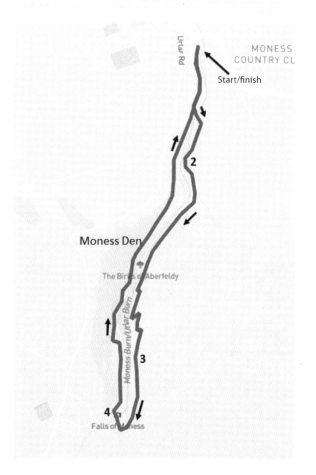

THINGS TO SEE AND DO NEARBY

Aberfeldy village has some great family-friendly cafes, including the one at the arthouse cinema in the centre.

Follow the River Tay to **Loch Tay**, one of the deepest in Scotland.

Visit the **Crannog Centre** to learn about Crannogs – the fascinating Iron Age roundhouses people once dwelled in on the loch – or hire a kayak and explore from the water.

Castles and Caledonian forests at Loch an Eilein

CAIRNGORMS NATIONAL PARK, SCOTTISH HIGHLANDS

Lying in the north of the mighty Cairngorm mountain range, near to the town of Aviemore, Rothiemurchus is one of the few remaining areas of the great Caledonian Forest that once covered much of Scotland. Stretching from the River Spey up on to the high plateau, the ancient forest – mainly of tall, slender Scots pines – is a haven for wildlife, carpeted with heather and blaeberry and home to rare capercaillie, pine martens, red squirrels and the Scottish crossbill, which is found nowhere else in the world. The trails through the forest cover some 30 miles (48km) in total and are perfect for exploration on foot or mountain bike.

Deep within the forest, Loch an Eilein (Scottish Gaelic for 'Loch of the Island') is a popular yet peaceful and intriguing place, surrounded by leafy forest and with a 14th-century ruined castle rising from an island in its centre. The castle was a stronghold of the 'Wolf of Badenoch' – Alexander Steward, Earl of Buchan. It was besieged by the Jacobites, retreating from Cromdale in 1690 and led by Dame Grizel Mor Grant, widow of the fifth laird Grant. Until the loch's water level was raised in

WALK DETAILS

Start/finish: Loch an Eilein Car Park, Rothiemurchus; grid ref NH896085, nearest post code PH22 1QT

Distance: 3.3 miles (5.3km)

Difficulty: 2/5

Public transport: Buses to Rothiemurchus, 3 miles (4.8km) from the start. Bike hire available from here.

SCOTLAND

the 18th century, the castle was connected to the shore by a causeway, but this now lies below the surface.

The trail around the loch makes an enjoyable walk on well-maintained paths with glorious scenery throughout and straightforward route-finding. The circumnavigation of Loch an Eilein as described opposite is just over 3 miles (4.8km), but an easy extension up to Loch Gamhna at the halfway point adds another 1.5 miles (2.4km) and explores a quieter and less-visited part of the forest.

On a warm day, there's no better way to cool off after a walk than with a paddle on the shingle beach at the finish. There are some good foraging opportunities along the route, too, including blaeberries in summer and the wood hedgehog – a pale-coloured 'tooth' fungus with spines rather than gills on its underside – in the autumn.

DIRECTIONS

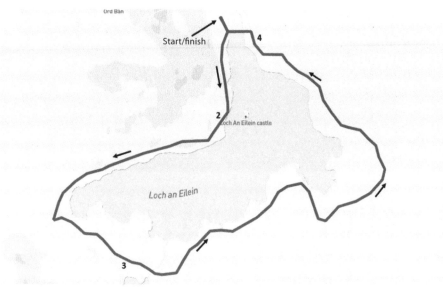

1 From the car park, walk straight towards Loch an Eilein, bearing right before the loch shore and following the clear path with the water on your left. You'll soon pass the island and castle on your left.

2 Go through the gate and downhill, continuing to follow the main path as it gradually winds its way around the loch shore.

3 At around halfway, just before a footbridge, the main path carries straight on. If you wish to extend the walk by 1 mile (1.6km), bear right here and follow the trail around the much smaller Loch Gamhna. This section gets muddy during wet weather. Otherwise, cross the footbridge and continue following the main trail around Loch an Eilein.

4 Shortly after passing the Forest Cottage on your right, follow the path around to the left, crossing a footbridge at the northern end of the loch. The shingle beach here is great for playing, or carry on past the beach and bear right to return to the car park.

THINGS TO SEE AND DO NEARBY

There's a shop at the car park, and a cafe and bike hire at the nearby **Rothiemurchus Centre**. This is a great place to wander around, with a farm shop and deli stocking lots of local produce for picnics – or if it's sunny, there's a lovely spot outside where you can sit with something from the cafe.

Neighbouring **Loch Morlich** is set in spectacular surroundings and the 3.75-mile (6km) circumnavigation is one of the most rewarding lower-level walks in this part of Scotland.

SCOTLAND

Explore the trails at Glencoe Lochan

GLENCOE, SCOTTISH HIGHLANDS

The dramatic surroundings of Glencoe are a real taste of higher, wilder Scotland as you head through on the winding A82. This landscape, with its towering mountains and rugged trails, is prized by those seeking higher, harder challenges. Glencoe Lochan, however, set at the far western end of the glen on the shores of Loch Leven and just outside Glencoe village, is an ideal introduction for mini mountaineers.

The lochan – meaning a 'small loch' – was created in the 1850s as part of a landscaping project by the then owner of the estate, the Earl of Strathcona, to make the area look more like the Canadian Rockies in order that his Canadian wife should feel less homesick. Today, it's managed by Forestry Scotland and is a peaceful place that's open for all to enjoy. There are three waymarked walks, which are ideal for all ages and abilities, in a breathtakingly beautiful setting.

The walks begin in the car park, where there's also a map of the routes. They are all about 1 mile (1.6km) in length and can be joined up to make a single, 3-mile (4.8km) walk. The red Lochan Trail is the main trail around the lochan and is accessible – look out for the friendly ducks along the way. The yellow Woodland Trail explores the nearby woodland and is more uneven and undulating, while the blue Mountain Trail is steep but offers great views from its high point, out across Loch Leven.

WALK DETAILS

Start/finish: Glencoe Lochan Car Park, Ballachulish, PH49 4HT

Distance: Up to 3 miles (4.8km)

Difficulty: 1/5

Public transport: Regular local and Citilink buses stop at Glencoe village

DIRECTIONS

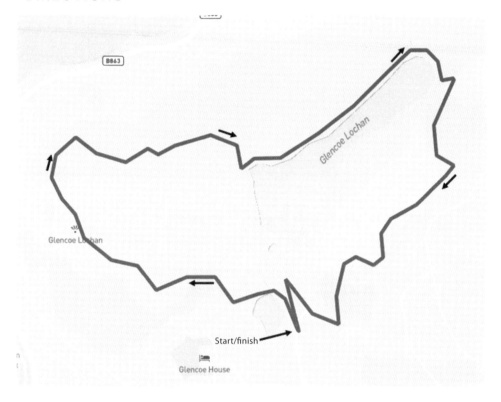

B863

Glencoe Lochan

Glencoe Lochan

Start/finish

Glencoe House

1 All three trails begin in the car park and are fully waymarked throughout.

THINGS TO SEE AND DO NEARBY

The Ice Factor – the National Ice Climbing Centre – in Kinlochleven makes a fantastic day out for budding mountaineers. Have a go at indoor climbing, or even indoor ice climbing, learn basic rock climbing skills, take on the aerial assault course and then refuel in the cafe.

Cross the silver sands at Camusdarach

ARISAIG, SCOTTISH HIGHLANDS

I t's hard to imagine a more perfect beach than Camusdarach, with its pure-white sands from where you can look out across the clear, blue sea to the rugged mountain skylines of Rum and Eigg. Set along the stretch of the coast known as the Silver Sands of Morar, these beaches can be linked up at low tide for a longer walk or simply enjoyed individually – it's easy to spend whole days at a time enjoying being there. Made famous in the 1983 film *Local Hero*, Camusdarach is an understandably popular place but if you can visit out of peak season – or, even better, go for a paddle before breakfast – you can often have this beautiful wide sandy sweep all to yourself.

At low tide, the lower shores of the beach are great for beachcombing. You might find brown wrack seaweed and rocks that are home to limpets, barnacles and whelks, as well as lots of interesting shells in some of the farthest bays. The white beaches in this part of Scotland are made from fragments of maerl, a type of seaweed, crushed by the waves and bleached by the sun.

This walk begins at the beach car park and heads straight over the dunes and on to the beach. After a loop of the sands, it heads inland, following gorse-lined trails back to the car park.

WALK DETAILS

Start/finish: Camusdarach Beach Car Park, Morar, Mallaig, PH40 4PD

Distance: Up to 3 miles (4.8km)

Difficulty: 1/5

Public transport: Morar train station is about 1.9 miles (3.1km) from the start

SCOTLAND

DIRECTIONS

1 From the car park off the B8008 by Glenancross, cross the footbridge following signs 'To the Beaches'. Turn right after the bridge and follow the path by the burn, keeping straight ahead to walk through the dunes and on to the beach at Camusdarach.

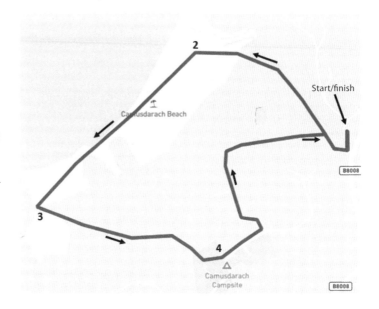

2 Head left across the beach to a rocky promontory at the far side. At low tide, you can walk around this but at higher tides you may need to scramble over it. Cross another section of beach and another promontory and walk as far as the grassy ground at the Rubha Dà Chuain Peninsula, which reaches out into the sea.

3 Head left up the wooden steps and through a kissing gate, following a path alongside a fence with the fence to your left. Go through the next gate and turn left on a path just before the woods that leads through gorse to reach Camusdarach Campsite.

4 Bear left, walking through the camping area and through a gate, turning left on to the drive beyond. Follow this between the farmhouses and on to a track, continuing straight ahead on to a grass path where the main track curves to the left. Go through a gate and follow the grass path through pine trees and down the hill to the footbridge by the car park.

THINGS TO SEE AND DO NEARBY

Nearby **Loch Morar** is a stunning place to visit, with enjoyable, easier walking from the parking area on the north-west of the loch. Or join a guided kayaking group at **Arisaig** to explore the intricate coastline, dotted with islands, where you can see seals and otters as well as many seabirds and interesting marine flora.

SCOTLAND

Around the Falls of Orrin

ORRIN, INVERNESS-SHIRE

Deep in the Highlands of Inverness-shire, the River Orrin rises in the East Monar Forest and winds its way east through the Strathconon and Corriehallie forests to its confluence with the fast-flowing River Conon near Dingwall. As the river passes to the west of Muir of Ord, it flows thorough a rocky gorge and down a series of steps known as the Falls of Orrin.

The adventurous trail that loops the falls is a great starting place for exploring the area, surrounded by wooded hills and accompanied by the rush of the water. It's also a great place to spot salmon leaping – legend has it that the highest salmon leap ever recorded, at over 11.5 feet (3.5 metres), took place here.

From the start, it's just a short walk upstream to the falls, where you'll find a series of rocky chutes and the remains of some historical hydro workings. There are some good shingle beaches for paddling nearer to the bridge at the start of the walk, which crosses the river to start and heads up the opposite side through Tower Wood. The Fairburn Tower that stands in the woods overlooking the Muir of Ord is a precious remnant of the Scottish Renaissance. Built in 1545 by the Mackenzie family, it has had a dramatic history and now stands in disrepair. However, the Landmark Trust is, at the time of writing, fundraising in order to restore this beautiful piece of architectural history.

WALK DETAILS

Start/finish: Parking area at Aultgowrie, Muir of Ord, IV6 7XA

Distance: 3.6 miles (5.8km)

Difficulty: 2/5

Public transport: Not easily reachable by public transport

DIRECTIONS

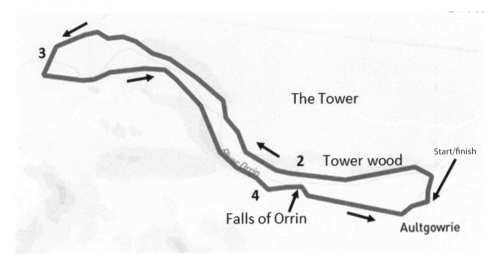

The Tower

Tower wood

Start/finish

2

4

Falls of Orrin

Aultgowrie

1 From the car park, return to the road and follow it north across the bridge to a gate on the left and a footpath into the woodland. Follow this along the northern bank of the River Orrin until you reach the falls and a path junction with Fairburn Tower to your right.

2 Continue along the riverside path until you reach some buildings and a bridge over the River Orrin.

3 Cross the bridge and turn left, following the minor road back along the southern bank of the river until you reach the top of a small hill, where there is a small path heading left and a cattle grid in the road.

4 Bear left and follow this path downhill to the weirs and Falls of Orrin, then continue on the path heading south-east slightly away from the river, across an area of newly planted trees and through a deer gate back to the minor road. Turn left and follow this back to the start.

THINGS TO SEE AND DO NEARBY

Head to the small town of **Beauly**, just to the south of Aultgowrie, with its castle, ruined priory and excellent selection of cafes.

Hills and Highland history in Balmacara

KYLE OF LOCHALSH, ROSS-SHIRE

Covering the rocky moors and wooded hills overlooking the Kyle of Lochalsh, Balmacara is a traditional Highland crofting estate. Rich in wildlife and history (the estate has been lived and worked on for millennia) yet peaceful and relatively undiscovered, ease of access and a great network of waymarked trails make it perfect for on-foot exploration.

This walk begins in pretty Balmacara Square, with its friendly cafe, gallery and visitor centre providing maps on the various walks. There's a good climb to reach the forested foothills of Sgurr Mor, from where there are spectacular views across Loch Alsh to Skye and the narrows of Kylerhea. Well-signed forestry tracks lead you to the quiet lane just outside the village of Reraig, from where there are inviting trails, accompanied by beautiful views, all the way to the short section of quiet road to finish.

Looked after by the National Trust for Scotland, the Balmacara Estate is an example of traditional Highland crofting: small-scale, low-intensity agriculture that benefits communities, the environment and a rich variety of native flora and fauna. As you wander through ancient, lichen-clad oak woods and dense pine forests, look for pine marten and red squirrels.

The beaches at Balmacara Bay and Reraig are covered in shells and a great place to watch seabirds, spot seals and perhaps even see otters, whales and dolphins.

WALK DETAILS

Start/finish: The Square, Balmacara, Kyle, IV40 8DP

Distance: 3.5 miles (5.6km)

Difficulty: 3/5

Public transport: Regular buses to Skye pass Reraig, at the halfway point of the walk

SCOTLAND

DIRECTIONS

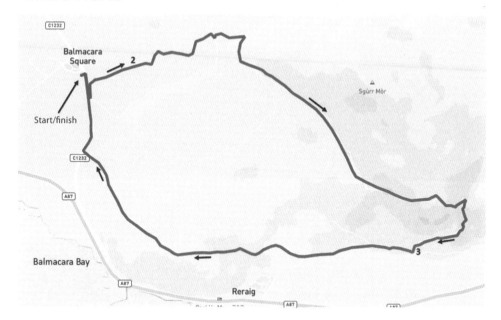

1 Turn right out of the car park and follow the lane south towards Reraig. After a short distance, turn left, following a 'forest walks' signpost into a field and alongside a stream.

2 Follow the path through a gate and steeply uphill on a gorse-lined path until you reach a wide forestry track. Turn left on to this and then take the next right at the blue-and-red marker, following the track through pinewoods and eventually descending past waterfalls to reach the road at Reraig.

3 Turn right and follow the road past the houses, bearing right on to the path where the road bears left towards Lochalsh. Follow this path over the hill, descending to reach a road. Turn right on to the road to return to Balmacara, turning left after the bridge back to Balmacara Square.

THINGS TO SEE AND DO NEARBY

Head over the bridge on to the beautiful **Isle of Skye**, with its jagged mountain ridges and unspoiled beaches.

Walk 100 at **Coire Lagan** is challenging but rewarded with spectacular views – and a cafe at the finish.

SCOTLAND

Crags and castles at Lochbuie

ISLE OF MULL, INNER HEBRIDES

The Isle of Mull is the second largest of the Inner Hebrides, after Skye. It's a place of vastly varying landscapes, from the rugged and mountainous central area, where Ben More rises to 3,169 feet (966 metres) almost straight from the sea, to the intricate, lengthy coastline and loch-studded lowlands. Tobermory, in the north of the island, is the main settlement, a colourful jumble of houses with a buzzing harbour and interesting shops. To the very south – the Ross of Mull – the landscape is more rolling, with several beautiful white-sand beaches, including Fionnphort and Ardalanish.

The village of Lochbuie lies at the head of the sea loch of the same name on the south coast of Mull, about 14 miles (22.5km) from the ferry port at Craignure. It is at the end of a long, quiet road that leads from the main A849 along the shores of Loch Spelve and Loch Uisg. Lochbuie is small but friendly, with an honesty shop next to the car park at the start of this walk.

There are many trails to explore here. The most spectacular one, which will keep children thoroughly entertained throughout its length, follows an out-and-back route along sandy beaches, past the mysterious Moy Castle and alongside some crags with intriguing caves. Moy Castle, standing on a rocky platform at the head of Loch Buie, was built in the 15th century by the Clan Maclaine of Lochbuie as a family home. Repair work has recently been carried out but access isn't permitted as it's still considered unsafe.

WALK DETAILS

Start/finish: Parking area at the head of Loch Buie, nearest postcode PA62 6AA

Distance: 2.5 miles (4km)

Difficulty: 2/5

Public transport: Ferries cross to the island from Oban, Lochaline and Kilchoan. Booking is often required on the Oban ferry.

DIRECTIONS

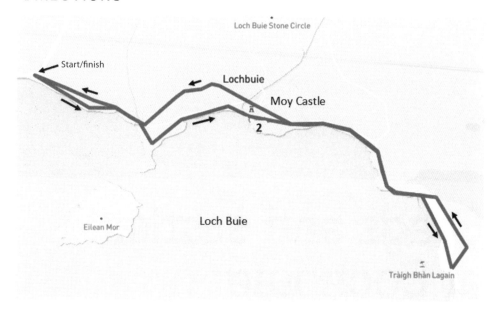

1 From the parking area, follow the coastline with the sea on your right. Depending on the state of the tide, you can either walk across the wide sandy beaches or along the clear 4x4 track that runs alongside the coast.

2 Pass Moy Castle and continue past some interesting rocky formations, then drop down on to the beach at Tràigh Bhàn Lagain. Follow this to its far end, then return via your outward route.

THINGS TO SEE AND DO NEARBY

Visit the beautiful white-sand beaches at **Fionnphort** and catch a ferry across to **Iona**. Look for otters and sea eagles hunting for fish.

Head north from Lochbuie to the **Ardmeanach Peninsula** on the west of Mull. There's an adventurous longer walk here, suitable for older children, which takes you out to the far end of the peninsula to discover a fossilised tree, over 39 feet (12 metres) high.

Sands and summits at Coire Lagan

ISLE OF SKYE, INNER HEBRIDES

The largest of the Inner Hebrides, the beautiful Isle of Skye is reached by bridge or ferry from mainland western Scotland. There's so much to explore here that it could easily fill its own book, from the beaches and rugged coastline and the lochs, falls and faery pools to the dramatic Cuillin Ridge that dominates the skyline.

Cradled in a deep bowl on the western edge of the Cuillin Ridge, Coire Lagan holds a tiny, magical loch. The first section of the walk up from Glen Brittle – where there's everything you need for a few days of incredible adventures, including a beach, a campsite and a cafe – is perfect for children. The brave and footsure can continue to Coire Lagan but it's still a challenging and enjoyable walk without this.

The route follows the main path up towards the summits, gaining height rapidly along a clear and well-maintained trail. Remember to stop regularly and take in the views behind you, out across the sea to the Small Isles of Eigg and Rum on the horizon.

Reaching the cairns higher up, the more straightforward route bears left, following a good path down past Loch an Fhir-bhallaich and the beautiful Eas Mor waterfall with its deep ravine and series of clear pools further down. The final stretch follows the road from Glen Brittle Memorial Hut back to the campsite. If you wish to make the out-and-back trip from the cairns, route-finding is straightforward but the terrain is much more technical and requires some scrambling.

WALK DETAILS

Start/finish: Glen Brittle, Carbost, Isle of Skye, IV47 8TA

Distance: 3.9 miles (6.3km)

Difficulty: 5/5

Public transport: Public transport trains to Fort William then Scottish Citylink coach to Sligachan on Skye

DIRECTIONS

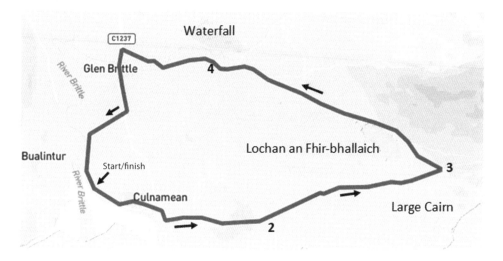

1 Starting from the cafe, follow the main path through a gate and east up the track towards the distant Cuillin Ridge.

2 Where the path forks after a short distance, stay left, continuing in a similar direction uphill and across a small stream. Continue up the path to a path junction marked with two large cairns, just before the ground becomes steeper. To miss out the technical section to Coire Lagan, turn left here and follow the descent path as described. To reach the coire, follow the steep, technical path out-and-back from this point.

3 Facing uphill, turn left at the cairns (bear right if you're coming down from the coire) and follow the clear path north-west below the slopes of Sgùrr Dearg and above Loch an Fhir-bhallaich. Continue on the path downhill to reach the grassy area above the Allt Coire na Banachdich and the impressive Eas Mor waterfall. Caution: take care at the edge of the ravine on this section.

4 Follow the path along the southern edge of the gorge, heading west downhill to reach a footbridge. Cross this and follow the grassy path to the road near to Glen Brittle Memorial Hut. Turn left and follow the road across the cattle grid and back to the start.

THINGS TO SEE AND DO NEARBY

Further north on Skye are the dazzlingly white coral beaches – actually formed from crushed maerl, a hard seaweed, rather than coral – and the black beach at **Carbost**, both of which are fantastic for exploring with kids, with great paddling and sea swimming.

INDEX

PICTURE CREDITS

All photos copyright Jen & Sim Benson except for the following: Alcott family – 6 (top), 107–109; David Wilson – 6 (third), 172–4; Robert Tilt – 7 (second), 56 (bottom), 89 (bottom left), 129–31, 175 (bottom), 176, 204 (top), 211 (left), 213 (left), 217–19; Zana Benson – 7 (third), 86 (right), 87 (bottom), 89 (top left), 157 (left), 183 (right), 187, 213 (right), 224–5, 243 (left); Alun Ward – 56 (top); Adam and Becky Lockyear – 60; Visit Isle of Wight – 61 (left); Sam Foggan – 61 (right); Yvette Woodhouse City of London Corporation – 87 (top), 88, 89 (right); Rebecca Lees – 186; Pembrey Country Park – 188–9; Wales Coast Path – 190; Tracy Purnell – 192–3; Mark Bullock – 209; Lisa Wells – 210, 211 (right); Chris Roxburgh – 212; summonedbyfells CC BY 2.0 – 246

Map data copyright OpenStreetMap contributors. Maps generated using www.gpxeditor.co.uk using imagery from mapbox.com

ACKNOWLEDGEMENTS

The research for this book has involved hundreds of walks with our children (first one, then two) over the past 9 years – our love and thanks to E and H for being such an incredible source of joy, creativity, inspiration and boundless energy. Thank you to Liz Multon at Bloomsbury for always offering such valuable and generous enthusiasm and feedback, and to Kate Beer at Bloomsbury for being brilliant to work with. Thanks to our families for unwaveringly supporting our endeavours. Special thanks to Joe & Zana; Lucy, Sam, Osker & Heidi; Rob Tilt; Mark Bullock; Alun & Faith; and the OS GetOutside Champs for help with this and past projects.